INTERACTIONS ACCESS

A Reading/Writing Book

Pamela Hartmann
Los Angeles Unified School District

James Mentel
Los Angeles Unified School District

D1316951

McGraw-Hill, Inc.
New York St. Louis San Francisco Auckland Bogotá
Caracas Lisbon London Madrid Mexico City Milan
Montreal New Delhi San Juan Singapore
Sydney Tokyo Toronto

an EBI book.

...ctions Access: A Reading/Writing Book

3 4 5 6 7 8 9 0 DOH DOH 9 0 9 8 7 6 5 4

ISBN: 0-07-026958-0

This book was set in 11/13 New Century Schoolbook by GTS Graphics.
The designer was Jane Moorman.
The editors were Roseanne Mendoza, Elaine Goldberg, and Celine-Marie
    Pascale.
The production supervisor was Tanya Nigh.
The cover was designed by Francis Owens.
The photo researcher was Judy Mason.
New line drawings were done by Ellen Sasaki.
R.R. Donnelly & Sons Company was the printer and binder.

Hartmann, Pamela.
    Interactions access : a reading/writing book / Pamela Hartmann, James
Mentel.
        p.   cm.
    ISBN 0-07-026958-0
    1. English language—Textbooks for foreign speakers. 2. English
language—Composition and exercises.   3. Readers—1950–   I. Mentel,
James.   II. Title.
PE1128.H384   1993
428.2′4—dc20   91-39457
                                                                CIP

Grateful acknowledgment is made for use of the following:

Photographs: *Page 42* © Celine-Marie Pascale; *59* © Celine-Marie Pascale;
78 © M.B. Duda/Photo Researchers, Inc; *80 (left)* © Celine-Marie Pascale;
80 (right) © Paul Conklin/Monkmeyer; *91 (top)* © Ken Martin/Impact
Visuals; *91 (middle)* © Peter Skrzypczak; *91 (bottom)* © Rick Gerharter/
Impact Visuals; *124* © Spencer Grant/Monkmeyer; *129 (top left)* © Diane
Rawson/Photo Researchers, Inc.; *129 (top right)* © Jean-Claude Lejeune/
Stock, Boston; *129 (bottom left)* © Owen Franken/Stock, Boston; *129 (bottom
right)* © David Powers/Stock, Boston; *140 (top)* © Kazuma Abe; *140 (middle)*
© Ira Kirschenbaum/Stock, Boston; *140 (bottom)* © Jesus Carlos/Impact
Visuals.

Realia: *Page 40* © 1991 Pacific Bell. All rights reserved. Portions of this
Pacific Bell bill have been copied and distributed by McGraw-Hill, Inc. with
the permission of the copyright owner, Pacific Bell. Pacific Bell is not
responsible for and assumes no liability for any loss, injury, or damage
which may be incurred by persons or entities using this Pacific Bell bill.
Any person or entity using this Pacific Bell bill does so at its own risk.; *51*
from the *New Horizon Ladder Dictionary of the English Language* by John
and Janet Shaw (New York: New American Library); *53* reprinted with
permission of Don Tech; *115* from *Just Around the Corner,* edited by M.
Weiss (New York: Cambridge University Press); *119 (top)* photo by Peter
Tyson/Earthwatch; *119 (middle left)* © Earthwatch; *119 (bottom right)* ©
Russ Schleipman; *124 (middle)* photo by Andrew Snedden/Earthwatch;
124 (bottom) photo by Elissa Ichiyaso/Earthwatch; *130* reprinted with
permission by MBTA; *144* and *146* with permission of Mastermedia Ltd.
for the excerpt from The Solution to Pollution by Laurence Sombke, © 1990
by Laurence Sombke.

CONTENTS

PREFACE

INTERACTIONS ACCESS: THE PROGRAM

Interactions Access consists of three texts, an *Instructor's Manual,* and an audio-cassette program for beginning-level students of English as a Second Language. The three texts are *Interactions Access: A Communicative Grammar, Interactions Access: A Reading/Writing Book,* and *Interactions Access: A Listening/Speaking Book.* The three are carefully coordinated by theme, vocabulary, language structure, and, whenever possible, by language function. A chapter in one book corresponds to and reinforces material taught in the same chapter of the other two books for a truly integrated, multi-skill approach.

Interactions Access: A Communicative Grammar. While this book is organized by grammatical structures, all chosen structures are presented, practiced, and applied in context. Grammar is presented in manageable sections, starting with simple material and gradually working up to more complex structures. In each chapter, students are led through a logical, complete presentation in which grammar points are consistently recycled and reinforced. Exercises following each grammar presentation proceed from controlled to open-ended. Like the other two books in this series, the grammar book includes a wide variety of communicative activities that are enhanced by art and realia. Through its conversational approach, the book helps students use the grammar structures they are studying in real-life communication.

Interactions Access: A Reading/Writing Book. The selections in this book, which were written by the authors especially for this audience, are carefully graded in level. While the readings are not difficult, the topics are more sophisticated than those found in most low-level readers. Vocabulary is recycled from chapter to chapter to provide reinforcement. Reading skills such as skimming, scanning, and finding meaning from context are emphasized to help students understand the structure and organization of each reading. To build students' confidence, chapters begin with highly controlled types of exercises and activities and build to freer, more communicative ones. The book is coordinated with the two companion texts in the Interactions Access program in terms of themes, structure, and vocabulary.

Interactions Access: A Listening / Speaking Book. This book uses lively, natural language from a variety of contexts. Listening materials include formal and informal conversations, interviews, lectures, announcements, and recorded messages. Speaking activities include role play, small-group activities, and classroom discussions. Listening strategies include making predictions, taking notes, drawing inferences, and listening for stresses in words, reductions, and intonation. A cassette-tape program is also available.

Interactions Access: Instructor's Manual. The manual provides instructions and guidelines for use of the three books separately or in any combination to form a program. For each of the three core books, there is a separate section with teaching tips, answers to the exercises, general activities, and a comprehensive sample test.

INTERACTIONS ACCESS: A READING/WRITING BOOK

Low-level academic English as a Second Language students are often frustrated by their lack of reading skills. Many are resigned to the belief that they will need to wait years before being able to read anything interesting in English. But this need not be the case.

The reading selections in *Interactions Access: A Reading / Writing Book* are intellectually stimulating but not beyond students' lexical, grammatical, or syntactic understanding. It should be noted that the reading selections—especially in the last few chapters of the book—*look* difficult but aren't. The level of grammar in these readings has been carefully controlled, as has the length of each reading. New vocabulary items can usually be guessed from the context, which has been meticulously constructed and for which there are follow-up exercises. Vocabulary items are recycled again and again, allowing students to absorb them easily. By the time students reach the last chapter, they will already be familiar with most of the words they find there.

At this level, it is difficult for some students to adapt to a very new method of language learning. If they are accustomed to the grammar-translation method of reading, they may be distrustful, at first, of this book, which emphasizes the importance of deduction by including practice in such skills as guessing meaning from context, making inferences, making predictions before reading, and learning to accept some amount of uncertainty.

Unlike *Interactions I* and *II,* the *Interactions Access* program combines reading and writing skills in one text. After completing Parts One and Two of any chapter (reading selections with exercises) and Part Three (scanning for information), students will have a firm base of vocabulary, grammar, and ideas needed for completing the writing exercises in Part Four. The time needed for any exercise in the book ranges from one minute to fifteen or twenty minutes.

CHAPTER ORGANIZATION

Each chapter is divided into four parts.

Part One: This section opens with artwork and prereading questions that set the tone for the reading selection that follows—a controlled nonfiction passage about the chapter theme. A postreading exercise is provided to help students check their general understanding of the reading selection and (in later chapters) of each paragraph. An exercise for guessing meaning from context is included, and some chapters contain exercises on making inferences, understanding pronoun references, noting details, and recognizing supporting material in a paragraph. Exercises for pair work or for small groups relate each reading to students' lives.

Part Two: Artwork sets the tone for the second controlled reading of the chapter. This reading is generally lighter than the one in Part One, and is usually fiction written in the first person. All chapters contain various exercises to help students expand their passive and active knowledge of vocabulary. In addition, exercises that relate the reading to students' lives are provided. Various study skills are stressed in this section to aid students in acquiring essential skills for academic reading such as following directions, dictionary usage, and understanding paragraph organization. Some chapters contain exercises that practice skills such as finding main ideas, details, categorizing, and using possessive pronouns.

Part Three: Advertisements, pages from brochures, bills, application forms, and so on are used to develop scanning skills. Some of this realia is, of course, simplified.

Part Four: Writing activities comprise this section. These range from controlled to freer activities and culminate with students composing a three-paragraph story about their lives.

ACKNOWLEDGMENTS

The authors greatly appreciate the ideas and advice of frontline teachers David Beaulieu, Dodie Danchick, Mynka Lewis, and Rochelle Weiss. Thanks also to our editors, Roseanne Mendoza, Elaine Goldberg, and Celine-Marie Pascale.

INTERACTIONS ACCESS

A Reading/Writing Book

1

NEIGHBORHOODS, CITIES, AND TOWNS

MONSTER CITIES

Before You Read

[handwritten: This city is large. It's not nice.]

Look at these pictures.

1. Is this city large or small? Is it nice?

2. What is the problem with this city? *[handwritten: Too Crowed Too many building No Trees]*

Read "Monster Cities." There are new words, but *don't use a dictionary.*

2

Monster Cities

A Are big cities wonderful places? Are they terrible? There are different ideas about this. William H. Whyte writes books about cities. He is happy in a crowded city. He loves busy streets with many stores and many people. He likes the life in city parks and restaurants.

B Many people don't like big cities. They see the large population of cities, and they are afraid. Many cities are growing very fast. They are "monster" cities. (A monster is a big, terrible thing.) In some countries, there aren't jobs in small towns. People go to cities to work; 300,000 people go to São Paulo, Brazil, every year. These cities are megalopolises. A megalopolis is a very large city. But now there is a new word in English—*megacity*. A megacity is a very, very large city. Mexico City is a megacity with a population of over 20,000,000. Tokyo-Yokohama is another megacity, with almost 30,000,000 people.

C There are problems in all cities. There are *big* problems in a megalopolis or megacity. In U.S. cities, there are many people with no jobs and no homes. The air is dirty. There are too many cars. A terrible problem is crime. Many people are afraid of crime.

D Population density is a big problem in megacities. Density is the number of people in every square mile. In Seoul, South Korea, there are 45,953 people in every square mile. Is this crowded? Yes! But in Teheran, Iran, there are 79,594 in every square mile. Do you think William H. Whyte likes Hong Kong? The population density there is 247,004!

Main Ideas

Circle the letters.

1. "Monster Cities" is about

   a. William H. Whyte.
   b. the number of people in American cities.
   c. the number of people in some very big cities.

2. Mexico City, Teheran, and Hong Kong are three

   a. small cities.
   - b. very big, crowded cities.
   c. cities with no crime or dirty air.

New Words

> It is not always necessary to use a dictionary to find the meaning of a new word. Sometimes the meaning of a new word is after the word *is* or *are* in the sentence.
>
> **Example**   Population is the number of people in a city or country.
>
> What is population? *the number of people in a city or country*

Answer the questions.

1. A monster is a big, terrible thing.
   What is a monster? *A big, terrible thing.*

2. A megacity is a very, very large city.
   What is a megacity? *a very, very large city.*

3. Density is the number of people in every square mile.
   What is density? *the number of people in every square mile*

Making Guesses

Circle the letter to complete the sentence.

The word *monster* is in the title ("Monster Cities") because

   a. the writer is happy in big cities.
   (b.) some cities are growing too fast.
   c. the air is dirty in some cities.

Discussion

Read this population chart with a partner. Then answer the questions together.

POPULATION OF LARGE CITIES			
WHAT IS THE POPULATION OF THESE CITIES?			
City, Country	**1991**	**2000**	**Density***
Tokyo-Yokohama, Japan	26,952,000	29,971,000	24,463
Mexico City, Mexico	20,207,000	27,872,000	37,314
Sao Paulo, Brazil	18,052,000	25,354,000	38,528
Seoul, South Korea	16,268,000	21,976,000	45,953
New York, USA	14,622,000	14,648,000	11,473
Teheran, Iran	9,354,000	14,251,000	79,594
Jakarta, Indonesia	9,588,000	12,804,000	122,033
Los Angeles, USA	10,060,000	10,714,000	8,985
Hong Kong	5,656,000	5,956,000	247,004

*Population per square mile

1. What is the population of Tokyo-Yokohama?

2. What is the population of São Paulo, Brazil?

3. What is the population of Mexico City?

4. What is the population density of Los Angeles, USA?

5. What is the population density of Seoul, South Korea?

6. What is the population density of Teheran, Iran?

7. What is the population density of Hong Kong?

8. What is the population of Hong Kong?

9. What is the population density of Jakarta, Indonesia?

10. What is the population of your city? Is it crowded?

PART TWO

MY NEIGHBORHOOD IN THE UNITED STATES

My Neighborhood in the United States

A My name is Etsuko Sasaki. I'm from Japan, but now I live in California. I'm a student here in English language classes at a small college.

B I live in an apartment building. It's on the corner of Olive Street and Sycamore Avenue. There's a big olive tree in front of the building. There's a park across the street. There are a lot of sycamore trees in the park. The trees are beautiful in the summer.

C A lot of my neighbors are from different countries. The people next to my building are from Indonesia. The family across from the Indonesians is from Colombia.

D The stores in this neighborhood are always busy. There's a Korean drugstore and an Armenian flower shop. A Chinese church is next to the flower shop. There are three restaurants on Olive Street: one Mexican, one Japanese, and one Moroccan-Italian-American!

E I like my neighborhood, but there is one problem. Where are the Americans?

About the Reading

Read Etsuko's story again. Then look at the map of her neighborhood. Answer the question about it.

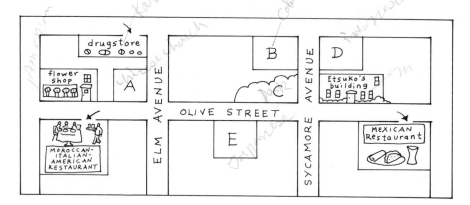

Where are these places? Write the letters on the lines.

___D___ Indonesian family's house

___E___ Japanese restaurant

___A___ Chinese church

___C___ park

___B___ Colombian family's house

Following Directions

Here are some directions from books and exams. Read these directions.

DIRECTIONS	EXAMPLES
1. Circle the word.	(building)
2. Copy the word.	street *street*
3. Underline the word.	building

4. Circle the letter of the answer.	Country:
	   a. summer
	   (b.) Japan
	   c. park

5. Fill in the blank.	My name *is* Etsuko.
6. Write the word on the line.	*neighborhood*
7. Correct the mistake.	co_ner

Follow these directions.

1. Circle the name of a city.

    Brazil   Indonesia   (Tokyo)   Egypt

2. Copy the name of a person.

    Mexico _____   California _____

    the USA _____   Etsuko _____

3. Underline the word for a building.

    I'm at a restaurant now.

4. Circle the letter of a kind of restaurant in Etsuko's neighborhood.

    a. Chinese   (b.) Mexican   c. Korean   d. Indonesian

5. Write the name of your country on the line. _____

6. Correct the mistake.

    C̶olombia

Building Vocabulary

A.   Write the words from this box on the correct lines.

church	Colombia	American	Japan
Italian	Mexican	apartment building	Korean
restaurant	elm	flower shop	Armenian
Indonesia	Indonesian	Moroccan	Japanese
sycamore	drugstore	olive	

COUNTRIES *Indonesia* , Colombia, Japan, _____

TREES *sycamore* , olive, _____

PERSON (OR THING) FROM A COUNTRY *Italian* , American, Korean, Japanese,
Indonesian, Moroccan, _____

BUILDINGS *church* , apartment, drugstore, flower shop

B. Fill in the blanks with these words.

front	√crowded	different	next	building	neighbors

1. This store is always _crowded_. There are always lots and lots of people.
2. There is a big apartment _building_ on the corner.
3. There is a school _next_ to my house.
4. My _neighbors_ are from Mexico. They're nice people.
5. There are two big trees in _front_ of my house.
6. People in my neighborhood are from _different_ countries.

Discussion

Talk about your answers in small groups.

1. What stores are in your neighborhood?
2. Are there people from different countries in your neighborhood? What countries are they from?

PART THREE

SCANNING FOR INFORMATION

Here is a Change of Address form. It's from the post office. When you move to a new house, apartment, or store, you need to complete a Change of Address form from the post office.

As soon as you know your new address, mail this card to all of the people, businesses, and publications who send you mail.

For publications, tape an old address label over name and old address sections and complete new address.

Your Name (Print or type. Last name, first name, middle initial.)
ANDERSON, PAUL

	No. & Street	Apt./Suite No.	PO Box	RR No.	Rural Box No.
Old Address	96 SYCAMORE AVE.				
	City	State	ZIP + 4		
	SANTA ROSA	CA	90012-3362		
New Address	No. & Street	Apt./Suite No.	PO Box	RR No.	Rural Box No.
	8962 ELM ST.				
	City	State	ZIP + 4		
	GREENWICH	CT	06839-0118		

Sign Here
Paul Anderson

Date new address in effect	Keyline No. (If any)
12/04/92	

PS Form **3576**, November 1990   RECEIVER: Be sure to record the above new address.

Circle the letters.

1. This new address is for

   a. one person.   b. a family.   c. a store.

2. The new house is in the city of

   a. California.   b. Santa Rosa.   c. Greenwich.

3. The person wants to receive mail at the new house on

   a. December 4, 1992.   b. November 20, 1992.   c. April 12, 1992.

PART FOUR

WRITING

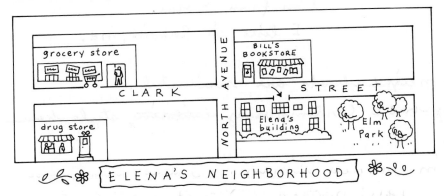

ELENA'S NEIGHBORHOOD

A. Answer these questions about Elena Paz and her neighborhood.

NAME: Elena Paz
FROM: Cuernavaca, Mexico
NOW: Chicago, Illinois
 student at Northwestern University

1. What's her name? _Elena Paz_ Where is she from? _Cuernavaca, Mexico_
2. Where is her home now? _Chicago, Illinois_
3. What is she? _student at Northwestern University._
4. Where is her apartment building? _on clark street_
5. What is next to her building? _Elm park._
6. What is across from her building? _Bill's Book store._

B. Now write a story about Elena Paz.

Her name is Elena Paz. She is a student at Northwestern University. She lives in Chicago, Illinois. Her apartment is on Clark street next to the Elma park. There is a Bills Bookstore across from her apartment a drug store is across from the grocery store. Both stores are on Clark street.

C. Answer these questions about yourself.

What's your name? My name is Karen Kins.

Where are you from? I'm from Korea.

Where is your home now? I live in Rockville, md.

What buildings are in your neighborhood? Where are they?
My neighborhoods are residental.
They have contemporary ~~building~~ style house.

D. Now write about yourself.

I'm married woman. When I was twenty three old. I and married. I met my husband twenty years old. We have been two Years later love affair.
Right now I have two daughters.
One is twenty years old and second daughter is seventeen years old.
They are both student.
We are lived in this hous five years.
I am not happy woman.
because I am all the time busy.
I ~~don't have~~ rest for a while.
must ~~sbathe~~

Punctuation

- Every sentence begins with a capital letter and ends with a period, exclamation mark, or question mark.

  This is my neighborhood.
    ↑   ↑

  capital   period

- There is a comma between a city and state or a city and country.

  San Francisco, California
  Jakarta, Indonesia
        ↑

       comma

- These words have a capital letter.

names of cities	São Paulo
names of states	Texas
names of countries	Iran
person or thing from a country	American, Korean
languages	Japanese
street names	Olive Street, Sycamore Avenue
people's names	Etsuko Sasaki
names of stores, buildings, and parks	Han's Drugstore
the word *I*	

E. Correct the mistakes.

      ^Mmy name is ^Nnikos ^Ssamarkis, ^Ii'm from ^Aathens ^Ggreece ^Nnow my home is in ^Ddallas ^Ttexas, ^Mmy house is on flower street^{.I} it is across from a ^{Ch}chinese restaurant, ^Ii'm a student at the school on the corner, ^Mmy classmates are from many countries, we're in an ^Eenglish class, ^Eenglish is necessary at school , because nobody there speaks my language

2

SHOPPING—A NATIONAL PASTIME?

PART ONE

IT'S A NEW WORLD OF SHOPPING

Before You Read

Look at these pictures.

1. Where is the woman in picture 1? What is she doing?

2. Where are the people in picture 2? What is the young man saying? What is the man answering?

Read "It's a New World of Shopping." There are new words, but don't use a dictionary. You will see the meanings of new words in parentheses — ( ).

1.

2.

It's a New World of Shopping

A   People are buying things in new ways these days. Many people are busy, and they don't want to go to crowded stores. They shop from mail-order catalogs (books with pictures of things to buy). Tired shoppers in some cities can even buy groceries (things in a supermarket) by phone!

B   Most people are shopping differently in stores too. They are taking groceries home in a different way. People in the supermarket ask, "Plastic or paper?" Many people like plastic bags, but plastic is terrible for the environment (the air, land, and water around us). Paper bags also are bad because we use too many trees to make them. Only five hundred bags come from each tree. Some people understand this. They aren't using plastic or paper bags. They're taking cloth bags to the store. These cloth bags are reuseable. (People can use them again and again for many years.) The bags are washable too. (People can wash them.)

C   Today many people are thinking about the environment. They want to have a safe world for their children. People are changing to different products (things in a store). Some mail-order companies are now selling special products too. Cloth shopping bags, cloth diapers (for babies to wear), and soap without chemicals help the environment. The mail-order companies help the environment and make a lot of money!

Main Ideas

Circle the letter of the main subject of "It's a New World of Shopping."

    a. shopping by phone
   ✓b. new ways to shop
    c. three kinds of bags in supermarkets
    d. new things to buy

New Words

> Sometimes a dictionary isn't necessary. The meaning of a new word is in parentheses — (   ).
>
> **Example**   They're using <u>mail-order catalogs</u> (books with pictures of things to buy).
>
> What are mail-order catalogs? *books with pictures of things to buy*

Answer the questions.

1. Tired shoppers in some cities can even buy <u>groceries</u> (things in a supermarket) by phone.

   What are groceries? *Things in a Supermarket.*

2. Plastic is terrible for the <u>environment</u> (the air, land, and water around us).

   What is the environment? *The air, land, and water around us.*

3. Cloth bags are <u>reuseable</u>. (People can use them again and again for years.)

   What can people do with reuseable cloth bags? *People can use them again and again for years.*

4. Cloth bags are <u>washable</u>. (You can wash them.)

   What can you do with washable cloth bags? *We can wash them.*

5. People are changing to different <u>products</u> (things in a store). *cloth shopping bags, cloth diapers, and soap without chemicals.*

   What are products? *Things in a store*

6. Cloth <u>diapers</u> (for babies to wear) are not bad for the environment. *help the environment*

   Who wears diapers? *For babies to wear. Diapers are use for babies.*

Details

Which things are good for the environment? Which are bad? Write *G* (good) and *B* (bad) on the lines.

1. *B* plastic bags
2. *G* cloth bags
3. *B* paper bags
4. *B* cloth diapers
5. *B* soap with chemicals
6. *G* soap without chemicals

Making Guesses

Circle the letter to complete the sentence.

The writer probably

    a. likes crowded stores.
    b. goes to the supermarket every day.
  ✔ c. wants a safe environment.

Discussion

Talk with a partner. Then share your answers with the class.

1. Do you use mail-order catalogs to buy things? *I wouldn't use mail-order often.*

2. Do you use plastic bags, paper bags, or cloth bags at the supermarket? Why do you use these? *I'm going to use cloth bags because for the environment.*

3. Do you know someone with a new baby? Does the person use cloth diapers? *My daughters didn't use cloth diapers. but I did use for my daughter*

4. What soap do you use for clothes? What soap do you use for dishes? What soap do you use for baths? Are the soaps safe for the environment? *long time ago. I'm going to try to use natural products the soaps because for the health to me.*

PART TWO

MY SHOPPING DAY

My Shopping Day

A I have a terrible problem. I love to shop. I go crazy in stores. Why is this a problem? Because I'm a poor college student. But I have an idea. I'm going to change the way I shop. There's a big store over there. I'm going to go in, and I'm *not* going to buy anything.

B Okay. I'm going in. I'm walking to the clothing department. Some people are just looking at things, but there are many people buying things. They're having a good time. Their shopping bags are full.

C I'm looking at some wonderful shirts. Oh! This one is my size, and it's a good color on me. I have some pants this same color. The shirt is washable too. I love it! And it's on sale! It's only $19.99!

D But I'm not going to buy it. I'm going to walk out of the clothing department. I'm going to walk out of the store. I'm *not* going crazy today. I'm *not* spending money today. This is wonderful! I'm so happy! How am I so strong today?

E My money is at home.

Following Directions

Here are some directions from books and exams. Read these directions.

DIRECTIONS

1. Cross out the word that doesn't belong.

2. Match the words. Draw lines.

EXAMPLES

wonderful

~~terrible~~

good

monster ——————— a place to live

apartment ——————— the number of people in a square mile

density ——————— a terrible thing

3. Match the words. Write letters on the lines.

_c_   the number of people   a. megalopolis

b. megacity

_a_   a very big city   c. population

_b_   a very, very big city

4. Put check marks next to things in the environment.

_✓_ air

_____ catalogs

_✓_ water

_✓_ land

Follow these directions.

1. Put check marks next to things in a store.

_✓_ groceries

_____ world

_✓_ shirt

_✓_ pants

_____ trees

_✓_ products

_✓_ clothing

2. Cross out the word that doesn't belong.

reuseable

washable

~~plastic~~

3. Match the words. Write letters on the lines.

_b_ groceries

_a_ again and again

_c_ mail-order catalog

a. many times

b. things in a supermarket

c. a book with pictures of things to buy

4. Match the words. Draw lines.

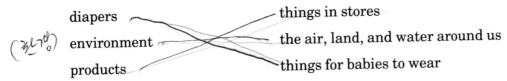

diapers   things in stores

environment   the air, land, and water around us

products   things for babies to wear

Building Vocabulary

A. In this box, there are six words for things in a store. Find them in the puzzle and circle them. There may be other words in the puzzle.

| bag | clothing | soap | shirt | groceries | product |

r	v	s	p	d	e	i	t	x	h	m	s
c	k	m	r	b	g	s	o	a	p	j	w
l	g	r	o	c	e	r	i	e	s	p	r
o	o	u	d	p	r	x	m	u	c	q	d
t	n	r	u	s	v	k	p	d	q	k	c
h	t	w	c	e	f	i	a	g	a	b	s
i	m	c	t	y	o	x	n	z	c	a	t
n	h	s	h	i	r	t	j	p	l	g	q
g	l	b	j	l	n	k	s	u	w	b	g

Understanding New Words: *-able*

Some words have two or three different parts. If you know these parts, you can understand a new word.

Examples

wash/able

wash   can   (You can wash it.)

re/us/able

again   use   can   (You can use it again.)

B.   Write a word with *-able* to finish each sentence.

you can wear it

1.   You can wear it. It is *wearable* .

2.   You can understand it. It is ___*understandable*___.

3.   You can like a person. He is ___*personable*___.

4.   The house is nice. You can live there. It is ___*niceable*___.

5.   You can love the baby. She is ___*babyable*___.

Discussion

Talk with a partner about shopping. Then share your answers with the class.

1.   Do you like shopping? Why or why not? *I like shopping always.*

2.   Do you like to shop alone or with a friend? *I like both way.*

3.   Some people go crazy in stores on a sale day. How about you? *I crazy to go shopping on a sale day*

4.   When are you going to go to a store? What are you going to buy there? *in stores.* *I like to go to a store anytime. I like to buy all kind of cloth.*

5.   Are there any differences between shopping in your country and shopping in the United States? *No differences between shopping in My country and shopping in the United States.*

PART THREE

SCANNING FOR INFORMATION

Mail-Order Catalogs

Look at this page from a mail-order catalog.

A. Write the letters of the words that mean the same.

1. a chemical   _c_
2. face   _e_
3. chili   _b_
4. insects   _a_
5. natural   _d_

a. ants, spiders, and so on
b. hot pepper
c. H_2O_4
d. no extra chemicals
e. front of your head

B. Match the words. Draw lines.

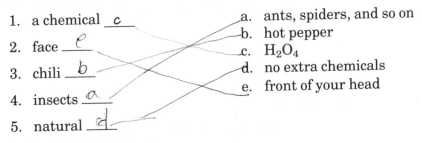

1. You're going to love this natural soap

2. You're not going to need five or six chemical cleaners

3. Insects are going to run away

4. You're going to say, "No paper or plastic"

because they don't like chili-garlic spray.

because there are no chemicals.

because you have a canvas shopping bag.

because Dr. Clean is safe and strong.

Using Order Forms

A. Here is the order form for Sunshine Products. Look at the picture of Joe and fill out the form for him.

Item	Code	Price	Quantity	Total $
natural shampoo	T6762	$3.00	3	$9.00
insect spray	D4545	$2.50	2	$5.00
canvas bag	A2104	$4.00	2	$8.00
hand soap	A2477	$1.00	4	$4.00
home cleaner	B2377	$2.25	1	$2.25
			Total Amount	$ 28.25

B. Now fill out this order. Use your name and address.

Karen   Kim   19832 Bothpage Ct.

first name   last name   street   apartment number

Ashburn   VA   20147

          city   state   ZIP code

total amount $ 28.25

PART FOUR

WRITING

A. What is Sue doing? Look at the picture and write sentences.

1. *She's walking into a department store.* ~~the~~
2. She's looking at ~~the~~ shirts.
3. She's buying the shirts.   She's paying for the shirts.
4. She's looking at the pants.
5. She's buying the clothes.
6. She's walking out the store.

Her bag is full!   She's going to her house.

B. Sue isn't going to the department store today. She's staying home and reading a book. Write four things Sue isn't doing today.

1. *She's not looking at blouses.*   She isn't walking into a department store.
2. She's not buying the clothes. She isn't looking
3. She is not walking out her house. at the pants.
4. She's not spending money.

She didn't spend a money.

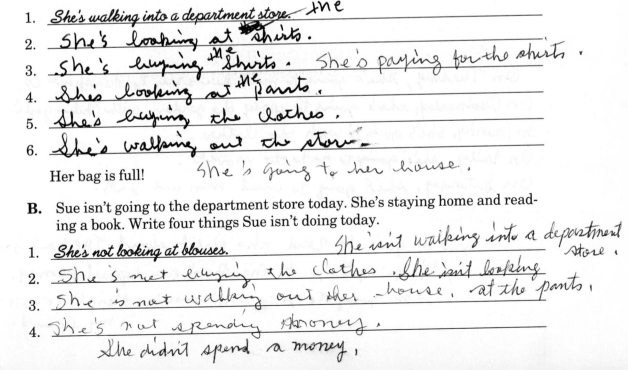

Writing Sentences in the Future

Sue is going to be busy next week. Here is part of her schedule.

MONDAY	TUESDAY	WEDNESDAY
buy cloth diapers	mail her order to Sunshine Company	spray the garden with chili-garlic spray

THURSDAY	FRIDAY	SATURDAY
wash the clothes	go to the movies	visit Mom and Dad

A. Write about Sue's week.

1. *On Monday, she's going to buy cloth diapers.*
2. On Tuesday, she's going to mail her order to Sunshine Co.
3. On Wednesday, she's going to spray the garden with chili-garlic
4. On Thursday, she's going to wash the clothes.
5. On Friday, she's going to go to the movies.
6. On Saturday, she's going to visit mom and Dad.

B. Now write about your week.

1. Tonight, I'm going to read the Novel about The Dark Son.
2. Tomorrow, I'm going to go to the Bank for deposit money.
3. This weekend I'm going to go to the movie Theather with my friend.

C. Now work with a partner. What is he or she going to do? Talk to your partner. Ask your partner about tonight, tomorrow, this weekend, and next summer. Then write sentences.

1. _Tonight my partner_ 's going to meet ~~the~~ his friend.
2. _Tomorrow my partner_ 's going to talk ~~the~~ with me.
3. _This weekend,_ He 's going to ~~travel~~ to the N. Y. City.
4. _Next summer,_ He is going to go to the ~~Pa~~ cific Ocean.

Just for Fun

Look at the picture. A man is crossing a bridge. Is the bridge going to break? He is carrying his groceries home. Is he going to get home? An alligator is in the river below. Is the alligator going to eat the man?

Write about what is going to happen. Use some of the words above.

bridge

alligator

Spray.
A man is going to walk the bridge.
He gets grocery bag. He needs walk to the over the bridge. Because his house is over there.
The bridge is very old. And an Alligator is under the bridge in water.
If the bridge is broken. He is going to die
But it's never happened.

An Alligator is very hungry ~~An A~~ because open ~~his~~ mouse
~~for~~ wait to the ~~foods~~.
he opens his mouse

FRIENDS AND FAMILY

CHANGING FAMILIES

Before You Read

Look at these pictures. Then answer these questions. Make a guess if you aren't sure of the answer. *there are five people in picture.*

1. How many people are in picture 1? Who is each person? *They are Nuclear family.*

2. How many people are in picture 2? Who are they? *There are three people in picture. They are single-parent family.*

3. How many people are in picture 3? Who are they? *There are fifteen people in picture. They are Extended family.*

Read "Changing Families." There are new words, but don't use a dictionary. You can understand some new words from the pictures.

1. Nuclear Family

2. Single-Parent Family

3. Extended Family

Changing Families

A Families in almost every country are changing. In North Africa, many people live in extended families. Fifty to a hundred people live together in a group of houses. These are all family members—grandparents, aunts, uncles, cousins, children, and grandchildren. But now this traditional family is breaking into smaller groups. Now there are more single-parent families.

B The traditional Japanese family is also an extended family—a son, his parents, his wife, his children, and his unmarried brothers and sisters. They live together in his parents' home. But this tradition is changing. Now most families are nuclear families. They have new problems. Most men spend a lot of time on the job. They don't see their families often. This is difficult. Many married women feel lonely. Their husbands are almost never home. Their children are at school. Sometimes these women get jobs or join cultural groups.

C In traditional European families, the wife stays home with the children. The husband has a job. Many Europeans aren't happy with this tradition. The number of divorces is going up. The number of single-parent families is going up too, and the number of marriages is going down. In Sweden, over 40 percent (40%) of all children have unmarried mothers. Also, many people live alone. In France, over 26 percent of women between age thirty and thirty-four live alone, and over 27 percent of men live alone.

D There are big changes in Quebec, Canada. In 1965, a traditional nuclear family was important. Almost 90 percent of men and 93.5 percent of women were married. But in 1985, only 49 percent of men and 51.7 percent of women were married! Now over one-third (1/3) of all babies have unmarried mothers. Over one-third of all marriages end in divorce.

E Some people are unhappy about these changes. But they need to understand one thing. We can't really say, "These new families are bad," or "These new families are good." They're just different.

Main Ideas

Circle the letters.

1. The main idea is

   a. in North Africa, families are big, but in Europe, they're small.
   b. families in many countries are changing.
   c. unmarried people are not happy.

2. The writer thinks that these new families

   a. are different from before.
   b. are good because they are small.
   c. are bad because people don't live together.

New Words

> Sometimes a dictionary isn't necessary. Sometimes a picture tells the meaning.

Look at the pictures on page 29.

Circle the letters.

1. An extended family is

   a. a family with a mother, father, and children.
   b. a big family with grandparents, parents, children, aunts, and uncles.
   c. a family with one parent and a child (or children).

2. A nuclear family is

   a. a family with a mother, father, and children.
   b. a big family with grandparents, parents, children, aunts, and uncles.
   c. a family with one parent and a child (or children).

3. A single-parent family is

   a. a family with a mother, father, and children.
   b. a big family with grandparents, parents, children, aunts, and uncles.
   c. a family with one parent and a child (or children).

Pronouns

What do these words mean? Circle the meaning of the underlined word. Then draw an arrow to it.

1. (Fifty to a hundred people) live together in a group of houses. These are all family members.

2. (Most men) spend a lot of time at their jobs. They don't often see their families.

3. (Many married women) feel lonely. Their husbands are almost never home.

4. (Some people) are unhappy about these changes. They need to understand one thing.

5. (The new families) aren't good or bad. They are just different.

Discussion

Talk about your answers to these questions with your classmates.

1. How many people are in your family? Do you live in a nuclear family, an extended family, or a single-parent family? Do you live alone or with a friend? *I have nuclear family. I live with my husband. My children were married 11 years ago.*

2. In your country, how are families changing? *My country is changed so fast. So I have six grandsons.*

3. Why are there more single-parent families in some countries? *The Tradition in Korea was in extended family. Now young gone The number of divorce is going up. They do not marry also.*

PART TWO

OUR FAMILY REUNION

Our Family Reunion

A This is a picture of my family. We don't live together. We live in different cities, but we often talk to each other on the phone. Every summer all the relatives come together for a week. This is our family reunion.

B In our family, people come to the reunion from Massachusetts, New Mexico, British Columbia, and Louisiana. One of my cousins flies to the United States from Ireland! We usually meet in a small town in Pennsylvania. My great-grandparents lived in this town.

C At the reunion, we have a picnic one day at a beautiful lake. We play baseball, swim, and eat a lot. We play volleyball too. The women and girls are on one team, and the men and boys are on the other. One night we always have a big barbecue. We sit around a fire, tell stories, and eat a lot. On the last night, we have a dinner dance at a nice hotel. We listen to music, dance, and eat a lot. Our family really likes to eat.

D We don't only eat. We visit with each other all week. We talk about problems. We plan weddings and cry about divorces. Sometimes we argue. Everyone brings their new babies, new wives and husbands, and new girlfriends and boyfriends.

E It's good to have a big family. But at the end of the week, I'm always *very* tired! I'm happy to be alone.

About the Reading

Answer these questions about the story. Circle the letters of the answers.

1. How often do these people have a reunion?

    a. every month
    ✓ b. every year
    c. every five years

2. How long is the reunion?

    ✓ a. one week
    b. two weeks
    c. one year

3. Why is a reunion important?

    a. because the people want to eat a lot
    ✓ b. because the family members live far from each other
    c. because the people want to visit Pennsylvania

4. How does the writer feel at the end of the week?

    a. unhappy
    b. hungry
    ✓ c. tired

Dictionary Use—Alphabetizing

Sometimes you need to use a dictionary. The words in a dictionary are in
alphabetical order—A to Z. It's important to know how to alphabetize quickly.
You need to look at the first letter of each word to put words in alphabetical
order.

Example   These words are in alphabetical order.
  alcohol
  diet
  food
  walk

If the first letter is the same, you need to look at the second letter too.

Example   These words are in alphabetical order.
  candy
  cigarette
  cup

If the first and second letters are the same, you need to look at the third letter, and so on.

Example   These words are in alphabetical order.

coffee

cola

company

1. Quickly, write the twenty-six letters of the English alphabet in order.

a *b* *c* *d* *e* *f* *g* *h* *i* *j*

k *h* *m* *m* *o* *p* *g* *r* *s* *t*

u *v* *w* *x* *y* *z*

2. Put the words in each box in alphabetical order. Number the words in each box. The first word is 1, the second word is 2, and so on.

3 every	
2 elderly	
4 exercise	
1 eggs	

3 golf	
2 gold	
1 glass	
4 gray	

2 remember	
1 relatives	
4 reuseable	
3 reunion	

4 full	2 environment
5 marriage	1 change
6 world	3 fire

4 together	5 traditional	3 guy
4 visit	2 group	7 very
6 trees	9 volleyball	1 groceries

_12_ special   _6_ cultural   _7_ hotel

_1_ almost   _9_ reunion   _2_ alone

_15_ cry   _3_ aunt   _4_ come

_9_ husband   _10_ safe   _11_ shirt

Building Vocabulary

In this box, there are words from the story. Fill in the squares of the crossword puzzle with these words.

parent	lot	divorce	fire	far
team	cousin	night	lake	eat
relatives	reunion	aunt	picnic	to

ACROSS

2. a group of people in a game

5. people in your family

7. your mother's or father's sister

8. Sometimes we eat lunch out-side. This is a _____.

10. something very hot (We can cook over it)

11. not day

14. a mother or father

DOWN

1. You can swim in a _____.

3. We need to _____ food every day.

4. the end of a marriage

5. a meeting of people after a long time

6. We eat a _____. (= much)

9. the child of your aunt and uncle

12. Every summer we go _____ a reunion.

13. He lives _____ from here. (= not near)

Discussion

In a small group, talk about families. Ask each person these questions. Fill in the answers on this chart.

Student's Name	Who do you live with?	Where do your rela-tives live?	How often do you visit your relatives?	Do you have family re-unions? When? Where?

PART THREE

SCANNING FOR INFORMATION

FURNISHED HOUSE (FURN HOUSE)

UNFURNISHED HOUSE (UNF HOUSE)

pets

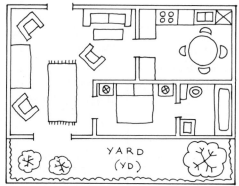

ONE-BEDROOM APARTMENT
(1-BD APT)

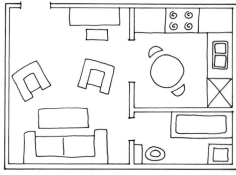

SINGLE APARTMENT (SGL APT)

SECURITY BUILDING
(SEC BLDG)

Understanding Housing Ads

Some people look at ads in a newspaper to find a house or apartment to rent. Read about the people below. Which apartment is good for each family (or person)? Write the telephone number from the ad on the line.

```
UNF HOUSE
3 bd, near schools,
 big yard, pets ok
 555-3211
FURN APT
1 bd, quiet bldg
555-6138
SGL APT
Furn apt, sec bldg
stv/frig, no pets
555-4826
UNF APT
2 bd, stv/frig,
w/pool 555-9277
FURN HOUSE
3 bd, near bus/
subway 555-6292
```

1. _555 – 4826_ A woman lives alone, but sometimes she is afraid. She doesn't have furniture. She doesn't have a stove or refrigerator. She doesn't have a dog or cat.

2. _555 – 3211_ A man and woman have two children and a dog. They have furniture.

3. _555 – 9277_ A man and woman have one child. They don't have a stove or refrigerator. They have furniture. All three family members like to swim.

4. _555 – 6138_ A young man and woman are married, but they don't have children. They are college students. They need to study hard. They don't have furniture.

5. _555 – 6292_ Three young men are friends. They are students in an adult school. They also work. They don't have cars or furniture.

Reading a Telephone Bill

Friends and family members sometimes live far from each other. The telephone is important to them. Look at this telephone bill. Then answer the questions about it with a partner.

PACIFIC * BELL™
A Pacific Telesis Company

Account Number	-4983 362 S 7184	Please Save For Your Records Check No: Date: Amount:	Page 1

Account	Previous bill	45.03
Summary	Payments applied through Nov 16	45.03CR
	Balance *** Thank You for Your Payment ***	.00
	Current charges:	
	Pacific Bell (Page 2)	29.21
	AT&T (Page 4)	5.54
	CURRENT CHARGES DUE BY Dec 14	**34.75**
Total Due		**34.75**
Late Charge Reminder	A late charge may apply on Dec 16 if your payment has not been received, however, your bill must still be paid before the DUE BY date to avoid any other penalties. (See Reverse)	
Whom to call	For billing questions call:	
	Pacific Bell	No Charge	811-7000
	AT&T	No Charge	1 800 222-0300
	When moving or placing an order call:	
	Pacific Bell	No Charge	811-7200
	The NEW 811 NUMBERS may not be available in your area. Call the Business office number on your bill or call Directory Assistance for an alternate number.	

1. How much is this telephone bill?   *It is $34.75.*

2. When does the person need to pay?   *The person has to pay until Dec Dec. 16.*

3. How much was the last bill?   *The last bill was $45.03.*

4. What number do you call if you want to ask a question about the bill?
    I call New 811   If I have a question about the bill

5. If you are moving, what number do you need to call?

PART FOUR

WRITING

> I often think about my family in Japan. I miss them, but I'm happy in California. Now I live with my aunt and uncle and two cousins, Sara and David. They're new in the United States too. They're from Peru. They don't speak Japanese, and I don't speak Spanish. I have to speak to them in English. Sometimes I don't understand them. Then we have to use pictures or sign language!

A. Write this same story about Etsuko and her new family.

Etsuko often thinks about her family in Japan. She misses them, but she's happy in California. Now she lives with her aunt and uncle and two cousins, Sara and David. They're new in the United States too. They're from Peru. They don't speak Japanese, and she doesn't speak Spanish. She has to speak to them in English. Sometimes she doesn't understand them. Then they have to use pictures or sign language.

B.   Answer these questions about yourself. Answer only one column.

I live with my family.

Where do you and your family live?

I live in Rockville, Md USA .

Whom do you live with?

I live with my husband and two daughters

What language do you speak at home?

We speak Korean at home.

Do you speak English at home? (never/always/sometimes)

We speak English at home Sometimes.

Where do you speak English?

I speak English to the work.

I don't live with my family.

Where do you live?

I live in Ashburn VA

Where does your family live?

My family live in Loudaun Co.

Do you miss your family?

No, My family live near in town.

Are you usually happy?

I'm always happy.

Whom do you live with?

I live with my husband now.

Do you speak English at home? (never/always/sometimes)

I speak English sometimes at home.

C. Talk with a partner. Ask this person, "Do you live with your family?" Then ask the person the questions from either column. Write the answers in complete sentences.

I live with my family.

Where do you and your family live?

I live in USA. and My mother used live in Korea.

Whom do you live with?

Now. I live with my husband and near by my two daughters family .

What language do you speak at home?

I speak Korean at home

Do you speak English at home? (never/always/sometimes)

Sometimes, I speak English at home .

Where do you speak English?

I speak English everywhere without at home .

I don't live with my family.

Where do you live?

_____

Where does your family live?

_____

Do you miss your family?

_____

Are you usually happy?

_____

Whom do you live with?

_____

Do you speak English at home? (never/always/sometimes)

_____

4

HEALTH CARE

GROWING YOUNG

Before You Read

the man washes T.V. sit in the chair
Look at these pictures. *He eats a Soda and chips.*

1. What is the man on page 45 doing?

2. Why is he unhappy? *He looks like unhappy.*

3. What things from page 45 do you do? *I'm doing exercise every other day.*
I am trying to eat healthy food all the time.
I'm studying when I have time.

Read "Growing Young." There are new words, but don't use a dictionary. You can understand many new words from the pictures. The meanings of other words are after a dash (—) or a comma (,). Sometimes an example helps you with a new word.

44

exercise

study

good food

meditation

Growing Young

A When many people are middle-aged—forty to sixty years old—they worry about their health. Some middle-aged people are afraid of old age. They don't want to be old, sick, and alone. On TV, they see athletes such as swimmers, baseball players, and tennis players. These middle-aged people would like to be strong, fast, and young again too, but they think they are "over the hill"—too old.

B Are they really too old? Maybe not! There are some interesting surprises these days. More and more athletes are still playing sports when they are middle-aged, and they're playing well. Mark Spitz won seven gold medals in the 1972 Olympics. He is still swimming, and he's over forty. Martina Navratilova, a tennis player, is almost forty. Nolan Ryan, a baseball player, and George Foreman, a boxer, are over forty. Arnold Palmer, a golfer, is almost sixty. Their faces aren't young. They have gray in their hair. But they are healthy and strong. How do they do it? Are they special, or can anyone be like them?

C Geriatricians—doctors for older people—are studying how people grow old. They're learning how people might be healthy at any age. First, it's important to exercise—for example, swim, walk, run, play tennis, dance, or play a team sport such as volleyball. Exercise is for everyone, not only young people. Second, people need to exercise their minds—to *think!* It's important at every age to study, read, and talk with people. Third, people need to eat a lot of vegetables and fruits and not much meat or sugar. Fourth, everyone needs to relax. People might try meditation! A 1989 study tells us something interesting. If older people meditate, they remember more and live longer!

D If you think you're over the hill, you should look around your neighborhood. Do you see that elderly woman? She's running down the street. Why are *you* just sitting there?

Main Ideas

A.   Circle the number of the main idea of "Growing Young."

1. Mark Spitz, Nolan Ryan, Arnold Palmer, and Martina Navratilova are very good at sports.

2. Some doctors study how people grow old.

3. If we want to be healthy, we need to exercise.

(4) People can be healthy at any age if they take good care of their health.

B.   Read the story again. Every paragraph has a letter. What is the main idea of each paragraph? Write the letters on the lines.

_3_ We need to do four things if we want to be healthy.

_1_ Some people worry about their health when they are forty to sixty years old.

_2_ Some athletes are still very good at sports when they are forty to sixty years old.

_4_ You can be healthy too, but it might not be easy.

New Words

Sometimes you can understand new words without a dictionary. The meaning of a new word is sometimes after a dash (—) or between dashes or commas (,).

Examples   When many people are middle-aged—forty to sixty years old—they worry about their health.

What does middle-aged mean? *forty to sixty years old*

Arnold Palmer, a golfer, is almost sixty.

Who is Arnold Palmer? *a golfer*

Look after the dash or comma in each sentence and write the meaning of the underlined word or expression.

1. They think they are "over the hill"—too old.

    What does *over the hill* mean? _middle-aged – forty to sixty years old._

2. Geriatricians—doctors for older people—are studying how we grow old.

    Who are geriatricians? _doctors for older people – are studying how we grow old._

3. We need to exercise our minds—to think.

    What does *exercise our minds* mean? _It's important everyone needs to exercise_
    for example, swim, walk, run, play tennis
4. Martina Navratilova, a tennis player, is almost forty.

    Who is Martina Navratilova? _a tennis player – is over forty._

Sometimes you can understand a new word because there is an example. Look in the sentence after the words *such as* or *for example*.

Example   We should eat healthful foods—for example, a lot of fruits and vegetables but not a lot of meat or sugar.

What are examples of healthful foods? _fruits and vegetables_

Write examples of the underlined words.

1. They see athletes such as swimmers, baseball players, and jockeys.
    Athletes are as swimmers, baseball plays, and jockeys.

2. We have to exercise—for example, swim, walk, play tennis, dance, or play a team sport. _Exercise the mean is swim, walk, play tennis, dance, or play a team sport._

Details

Which things should people do if they want to be healthy? Put check marks on the lines.

1. _✓_ study
2. ___ smoke
3. _✓_ exercise
4. _✓_ eat vegetables

5. ___ eat a lot of sugar
6. _✓_ talk with people
7. _✓_ relax

Discussion

Talk about health in small groups. *I like to exercise – I swim every other day.*

1. Do you like to exercise? Do you play any sports? If so, which ones? How often?

2. What sports would you like to play?

3. Are you afraid of old age? What do you do to be healthy?

I like to play swim for every day.

I'm afraid of old aged but I do to eat healthy foods, exercise, and study for every day.

PART TWO

ARE YOU HEALTHY?

Are You Healthy?

Most of us don't really want to be Olympic swimmers or baseball players. But we want to be healthy when we're young, middle-aged, and elderly. Take this test. It will answer the question, Am I healthy? Circle the letters of your answers.

1. Do you eat foods with sugar, such as candy, donuts, and ice cream?

   a. never   b. sometimes   c. often

2. Do you eat a *good* breakfast every day, not just coffee and a donut?

   a. yes   b. usually   c. no

3. Do you eat fruits and vegetables every day?

   a. 5 or more   b. 1 or 2   c. no

4. Do you smoke?

   a. never
   b. 1–10 cigarettes every day
   c. 10+ cigarettes every day

5. Do you drink coffee or cola?

    a. no
    b. 1–2 cups or glasses every day
    c. 3–10 cups or glasses every day

6. Do you sleep 7–8 hours every night?

    a. yes   b. no

7. Are you overweight?

    a. no   b. 5–19 pounds   c. 20–50 pounds

8. How far do you walk every day?

    a. 1–5 miles   b. ½–1 mile   c. 0 miles

9. How often do you eat eggs?

    a. seldom or never
    b. 2–3 times every week
    c. every day

10. Do you exercise (run, swim, play a
    team sport)?

    a. often
    b. 1 time every week
    c. seldom or never

11. How much alcohol do you drink every week?

    a. 0–7 glasses   b. 8–15 glasses   c. 16+ glasses

12. Do you worry, or are you unhappy?

    a. seldom   b. sometimes   c. often

How healthy are you?

> Every answer a. = 3.
> Every answer b. = 2.
> Every answer c. = 0.
>
> YOUR SCORE: _____
> 30–36 = You're probably very healthy.
> 25–29 = You might need to make some changes.
> 0–24 = You might not be healthy.

Discussion

Work with a partner. Look at your answers and your partner's answers to the questions on pages 49 and 50. Give your partner advice. Use *should* and *shouldn't.*

Dictionary Use—Guide Words

Sometimes you can't understand a new word without a dictionary. If you want to find a word fast, you need to use guide words. Guide words are at the top of every dictionary page, usually in the left and right corners.

Example   Here is a dictionary page. The guide words are *picnic* and *pig.*

---

picnic	386	**pig**

picnic (4) [pik'nik], *n.* a meal planned for eating outdoors. **Ex.** *They ate their picnic beside the river.* —*v.* have a picnic. **Ex.** *We picnicked in the woods.* —**pic'nick·er**, *n.* **Ex.** *After lunch, the picnickers made up teams for a game of baseball.*

picture (1) [pik'čər], *n.* 1. a painting, drawing, or photograph. **Ex.** *That picture of the President is seen often in the newspaper.* 2. that which strongly resembles another; an image. **Ex.** *She is the picture of her mother.* 3. a description. **Ex.** *The author gives a lively picture of his life as a sailor.* 4. a motion picture; movie. **Ex.** *The whole family enjoyed the picture we saw last night.* —*v.* describe. **Ex.** *The speaker pictured the scene in colorful words.* —**pic·tor'i·al**, *adj.*

pie (2) [pay'], *n.* a baked dish consisting of a thin shell, and sometimes a cover, made of flour and cooking oil and filled with fruit, meat, etc. **Ex.** *She put the pie in the oven to bake.*

piece (1) [piys'], *n.* 1. an amount or a part considered as an individual unit. **Ex.** *Please give me a piece of writing paper.* 2. a part taken away from something larger. **Ex.** *She cut the pie into six pieces.* 3. a coin. **Ex.** *Can you change this fifty-cent piece?* —*v.* join together; make whole. **Ex.** *She pieced together the broken dish.* —**go to pieces**, become upset or excited. **Ex.** *He goes to pieces when I disagree with him.*

piecemeal [piys'miyl'], *adv.* one part at a time; piece by piece. **Ex.** *He put the machine together piecemeal in his spare time.*

piecework [piys'wərk'], *n.* work paid for by the piece finished instead of by the hour, day, etc. **Ex.** *She does piecework at home.*

pier (3) [pi:r'], *n.* a structure built over the water and used as a landing place for ships and boats. **Ex.** *The ship is at pier seven.*

pierce (4) [pirs'], *v.* 1. break into or through. **Ex.** *The knife had pierced the wall.* 2. make a hole or opening in. **Ex.** *Many girls have their ears pierced for earrings.* 3. force a way through. **Ex.** *They tried to pierce the enemy's defense.* 4. deeply or sharply affect the senses or feelings. **Ex.** *They were pierced by the icy winds.*

pig (2) [pig'], *n.* a farm animal with a broad nose and fat body, raised for its meat.

· PIG

The first word on this page is *picnic*. The last word is *pig*. The words on a dictionary page come between these two guide words. You just need to look at the guide words, and you'll know if your new word is on this page.

A.   Use your dictionary. Find these pages quickly. What are the guide words? Write them here.

1. page 32 _____   _____

2. page 196 _____   _____

3. page 15 _____   _____

4. page 203 _____   _____

5. page 78 _____   _____

B.   Can you find the words on the left on dictionary pages with the guide words on the right? Write *yes* or *no* on each line.

                                                  GUIDE WORDS

1. *no* swim   sleep—smoke

2. ____ fact   face—fan

3. ____ nice   never—night

4. ____ long   learn—listen

5. ____ overweight   old—pitcher

6. ____ grow   gray—health

7. ____ store   still—sugar

8. ____ young   vegetable—walk

C.   Now use your dictionary to find these words. Use the guide words in the dictionary for help. Write the page number for each word.

WORD	PAGE	WORD	PAGE	WORD	PAGE
interesting	____	message	____	noise	____
meditate	____	attack	____	serious	____
noise	____	emergency	____	heart	____

Building Vocabulary

Cross out the word that does not belong in each group.

1. brother ~~friend~~ cousin sister

2. fruits meat vegetables ~~glass~~

3. baseball golf ~~dance~~ volleyball

4. cola alcohol coffee ~~candy~~

5. ~~overweight~~ young old middle-aged

6. think walk learn ~~remember~~

7. ~~fish~~ donut candy ice cream

8. difficult unhappy terrible ~~begin~~

PART THREE

SCANNING FOR INFORMATION

Using Emergency 911

Read this page from the phone book.

Emergency numbers

FIRE
POLICE **9-1-1**

Also call 9-1-1 for emergency ambulance service and for street accidents involving personal injury.
Non-emergencies   744-4000

Or
dial "0" (Operator)
in any emergency

If you cannot stay at the telephone, tell the operator the exact location where help is needed.

Números de emergencia

INCENDIO
POLICIA **9-1-1**

Use este número también para servicios de ambulancia en casos de emergencia y para reportar accidentes en la calle que comprendan perjuicio personal.
Llamadas no muy urgentes   744-4000

En caso de
cualquier emergencia
marque "0" (operadora)

Si ud no puede permanecer en el teléfono, diga al telefonista la dirección exacta donde se necesita ayuda.

Emergency Assistance for Deaf Persons

Telecommunications Device for the Deaf (TDD) emergency and non-emergency numbers:

Chicago Fire   744-9110 (TDD only)
Chicago Police   922-1414 (TDD only)

Illinois Relay Center
Non-Emergency Calls Only   1-800-526-0844 (TDD only)
or 1-800-526-0857 (Voice)

The phrase (TDD only) after a directory listing indicates the telephone is answered using a Telecommunications Device for the Deaf, and communication can take place only with another TDD. If a listing is followed by (TDD and Voice), both TDD-users and speaking/hearing people can communicate over the line.

Warning: Illinois law defines harassment as the use of the telephone to make lewd or indecent comment or request with intent to offend .... to abuse, threaten or harass (whether conversation takes place or not) .... to cause another's telephone to ring repeatedly with intent to harass .... to knowingly allow one's telephone to be used for any of these purposes. The law provides a penalty of up to six months in jail and a $500 fine.

Your Doctor

Office _____

Home _____

Ambulance

See Ameritech Pages Plus ™ Yellow Pages under "Ambulance Service"

Federal Bureau of Investigation
431-1333

U.S. Secret Service
353-5431

Coast Guard Rescue
353-0278

To Report
Seeing a Tornado:
• In Chicago, call 9-1-1.
• Outside Chicago, call the local Police, Sheriff or State Police.
Reports will be relayed to the responsible National Weather Service.

© The Reuben H. Donnelley Corporation 1991

A. Look at the questions and read about the problem. Answer the questions.

1. Is this an emergency or a nonemergency?
   It's an emergency.

2. Should he call 911?
   Yes, he should.

3. Is this an emergency or a nonemergency?
   It's an emergency.

4. Should she call 911?
   Yes, she should.

5. Is this an emergency or a nonemergency?
   It's an emergency.

6. Should he call 911?
   Yes, he should.

7. Is this an emergency or a nonemergency?

   It's an emergency.

8. Should she call 911?

   Yes, she should.

B. Work with a partner. Ask questions about calling 911. Your partner will answer "Yes, you should," or "No, you shouldn't."

Example   STUDENT A: The apartment is on fire! Should I call 911?
   STUDENT B: Yes, you should.

Reading Get-Well Cards

*Hoping
you're better soon*

We hope
that someone dear to us
will feel as good as new,
someone who means
a lot to us –
a special someone – you.

*Get well!
Angie*

A. George is sick. He's in the hospital. This is a card from his friends at work. Many people write little messages when they sign a card. Sign your name on the card. Write one of the following messages to George.

   Get well soon, George.
   You're special.
   Hope to see you soon.

B.   Read the poem on the card. Write the letters of the words from the poem that mean the same.

1. "dear to us" _*b*_   a. George

2. "as good as new" ____   b. we like you very much

3. "a special someone" _*d*_   c. okay again, healthy again

4. "you're better" ____   d. in a short time

5. "soon" ____   e. you're healthy

Understanding Medicine Labels

George has a lot of health problems. Here are some of the medicines he must take every day. Read the directions for each medicine.

a. Take two tablets in the morning.
TAKE WITH FOOD

b. Take one capsule after every meal.

c. Take one teaspoonful before bed.

d. Take two tablespoonfuls four times a day.
DO NOT TAKE WITH FOOD

A.   Now match the type of medicine with the time George must take the medicine. Write the letters of the pictures on the lines.

1. _*b*_   He ate a meal.

2. _*a*_   He is eating breakfast.

3. _*d*_   He is at work.

4. _*c*_   He is going to sleep.

B.   Now complete these directions for George using the information on page 56.

1. *George must take two tablets with food in the morning.*

2. *George must take one capsule after every meal.*

3. *He must take one teaspoonful before bed.*

4. *He must take two tablespoonfuls four times a day,
     without meal.*

PART FOUR

WRITING

Using *Or* and *So*

Or = (I'll only do one thing.)
   Use *or* when you make a choice between two things.

   Tonight I might read.   Tonight I might study.

or

   Tonight I might read, or I might study.

So = (That's why.)

   I exercise.   (That's why)   I'm healthy.

so

   I exercise, so I'm healthy.

Connect the pairs with *or* and *so*. Use a comma (,) before *or* and *so*.

1.   You can study. You can talk with people.

   You can study, or you can talk with people.

2.   People want to relax. They meditate.

   people want to relax, so they meditate.

3. Are some athletes over the hill? Are they still playing?

Are some athletes over the hill, so are they still playing?

4. Athletes work hard. They can still play.

Athletes work hard, so they can still play.

5. You can swim. You can play tennis.

You can swim, so you can play tennis.

Using *Should* and *Shouldn't*

A. George is still not very healthy. He needs some advice. Here are his problems. Write advice for him. Use *He should* or *He shouldn't.*

1. George never exercises.

He should exercise.

2. George drinks a lot of coffee.

George shouldn't drink a lot of coffee.

3. George never relaxes.

George should relax.

4. George smokes.

George shouldn't smoke.

5. George drinks a lot of alcohol.

George shouldn't drink a lot of alcohal.

6. George never eats fruits and vegetables.

George should eat fruits and vegetables.

B. Now write four sentences of advice for yourself.

1. I should *exercise*

2. I should *eat fruits and vegetables.*

3. I shouldn't *drink a lot of coffee.*

4. I shouldn't *drink a lot of alcahal.*

Using *Will* and *Won't*

Every New Year, George writes a promise to himself. Here is his promise this year.

This year I will be healthier. I won't eat donuts every morning. I won't drink six cups of coffee a day—I'll only drink one. I won't smoke. I will sleep eight hours every night. I will try to relax. I will walk two miles every day. And most of all, I won't worry about anything!

Now write about your promises for next year. Use *I will* and *I won't*.

Next year I'll be healthier, I'll eat a lot of fruits and vegetables. I won't eat junk foods, cakes, candys, cakes, and donuts. I'll drink only one cup of coffee in the morning. I won't drink alcoholic every night befor sleep. I'll exercise a lot, swim, arobic, run, and walk. I'll relax. I'll study a lot, read newspaper, English, and talk to my friend.

MEN AND WOMEN

MEN'S TALK AND WOMEN'S TALK IN THE UNITED STATES

Before You Read

Look at the pictures and the people's words on page 61.

1. In 1, the man doesn't understand something. What is it?

2. In 1, the woman is a little angry. Why?

3. In 2, the woman is unhappy. Why?

4. In 2, the man is unhappy. Why?

5. Do men and women talk in different ways?

> When you read "Men's Talk and Women's Talk in the United States," don't use a dictionary. Use pictures, examples, and words in parentheses to understand new words. Also, you'll learn to find the meaning of a new word after the phrase, *in other words*.

1.

2.

Men's Talk and Women's Talk in the United States

A   Marriage often is not easy. Love often is not easy. Sometimes friendship between a man and a woman is not easy. Maybe a man and a woman love or like each other, but they argue. They get angry. Later they apologize (say "I'm sorry"), but it happens again and again. What's the problem? Are men and women really very different?

B   Deborah Tannen says yes. Men and women *are* very different. Tannen teaches at Georgetown University. She writes books about the ways people talk. She believes that men and women talk—and think—in different ways. She tells about some differences in her book *You Just Don't Understand.*

C   The differences, Tannen says, begin when men and women are children. Very young boys and girls are similar to each other. In other words, they like the same things and play in the same ways. They aren't very different. But then there is a change.

D   When children in the United States are five or six years old, boys usually play in large groups. One boy gives orders. For example, he says, "Take this," "Go over there," and "Be on this team." He is the leader. Boys also brag. In other words, they say good things about themselves. They do this to have a high position. Position in the group is important to boys.

high position   ↑

low position   ↓

E   Girls in the United States usually play in small groups or with one other girl. A girl's "best friend"—her very, very good friend—is important to her. Girls don't often give orders; they give suggestions. For example, they say, "Let's go over there," "Maybe we should do this," and "Do you want to play with that?" Girls don't usually have a leader, and they don't often brag. Everyone has an equal position.

equal positions   ←——→

F   Little boys are usually active; they *do* things. Much of the time, little girls sit together and talk. When children grow up, nothing really changes. Men usually do things together. Or they talk about *activities* such as sports and *things* such as cars and world problems. They talk to give or get information. But for women, *people* and *feelings* are important. Women often talk to show interest and love. Although a man and woman speak the same language, sometimes they don't understand each other. Men's talk and women's talk are almost two different languages. But maybe men and women can learn to understand each other if they understand the differences in speech.

Main Ideas

Which sentences are about men? Which sentences are about women? Write *M* (men) and *W* (women) on the lines.

1. __M__ When they are children, they usually play in large groups.
2. __W__ When they are children, they usually play in small groups or with one friend.
3. __W__ There usually isn't a leader in the children's play group.
4. __M__ One child in the play group is the leader.
5. __W__ They talk to show interest and love.
6. __M__ They talk to give or get information.

Discussion

Talk with a small group about your answers to these questions.

1. When you were a child, did you play in a big group or a small group? Did you have a best friend?   *I played in a small group, I had a best friend when I was a child.*
2. Would you like to have a high position in a group, or would you like to be in a group with equal positions?   *I would like to to be in a group with equal position when I was child.*
3. What do you sometimes argue about with your husband? wife? boyfriend? girlfriend?   *I did argue about with my husband all the times.*
4. In your country, do men and women talk differently? If so, give examples.   *Yes, my country, men and women talk differently. In For example. Men want to play a golf but women want to go to shopping.*

New Words

A.   Use the examples and the words in parentheses to understand these words. (The large letters in parentheses are paragraphs from page 62.) Write letters on the lines.

1. __b__ apologize (A)

2. __c__ orders (D)

3. __e__ position (D)

4. __a__ suggestions (E)

5. __d__ equal (E)

a. ideas ("Maybe we should do this.")
b. to say "I'm sorry."
c. commands ("Do this.")
d. same
e. place in a group

Sometimes you can understand a new word because the meaning is after the phrase *in other words.*

Example   He wanted to become a geriatrician; in other words, he hoped to become a doctor for elderly people.

What does *geriatrician* mean?   *a doctor for elderly people*

B.   Look after the phrase *in other words.* Finish the definition (meaning) of the underlined words.

1. They are very similar. In other words, they like the same things and play in the same way. They aren't very different.

   Similar means not __very different__ .

2. Boys brag; in other words, they say good things about themselves.

   When people brag, they say __good things about themselves__ .

3. Little boys are usually active; in other words, they do things.

   Active people don't sit and do nothing. They __do things__ .

PART TWO

HE SAID/SHE SAID: A U.S. COUPLE

He Said/She Said: A U.S. Couple

A   Well, Doctor, I'm beginning to worry about my marriage. My wife and I just don't understand each other. She doesn't like to do things with me. She won't play tennis or baseball with me. She doesn't like to fix the car with me. She doesn't work on the house with me—you know, paint the house or fix the roof. She doesn't listen when I talk about interesting things: sports, money, or world politics. Sometimes she gets angry with me about unimportant things. And she talks and talks and talks about uninteresting things. What's wrong with her?

B   Well, Doctor, I'm beginning to worry about my marriage. My husband and I just don't understand each other. We both work full-time, but I do all the work at home—you know, fix dinner, wash clothes, and clean the house. His life is easy; he has only one job. I have two! Sometimes I feel so lonely. When he's home, he reads the newspaper or watches TV. He doesn't talk *with* me; he talks *at* me. He only talks with his friends. He doesn't listen if I tell him about my day. He isn't interested in our friends and relatives. Sometimes he gives me orders. Sometimes he tells me about sports or politics, but I don't like it because I feel like a student in school. What's wrong with him?

About the Reading

The man is unhappy about many things. What does he say? Put checks on the lines.

1. __✓__ His wife doesn't like to do things with him.

2. __✓__ His wife talks about uninteresting things.

3. _____ His wife gives him orders.

4. __✓__ His wife doesn't listen when he talks about sports, money, or politics.

The woman is unhappy about many things. What does she say? Put checks on the lines.

1. _____ Her husband gets angry about unimportant things.

2. __✓__ She goes to work and does all the work at home too.

3. _____ Her husband doesn't talk with her.

4. __✓__ Her husband gives her orders.

Reading Speed

Students usually need to read fast because they have to read many books each year. Also, they can understand more if they read fast.

Examples

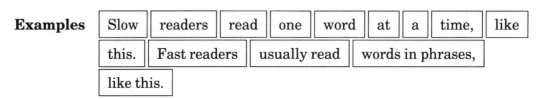

| Slow | readers | read | one | word | at | a | time, | like |
| this. | Fast readers | usually read | words in phrases, |
| like this. |

Read these sentences in phrases. Read silently; in other words, do not speak.

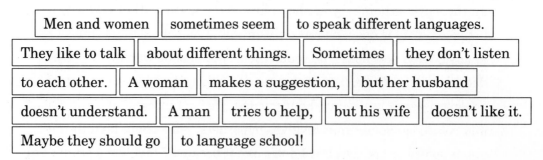

Men and women	sometimes seem	to speak different languages.
They like to talk	about different things.	Sometimes	they don't listen
to each other.	A woman	makes a suggestion,	but her husband
doesn't understand.	A man	tries to help,	but his wife	doesn't like it.
Maybe they should go	to language school!

Building Vocabulary

A.   Complete these sentences. Circle the letters of the answers. There is one answer for each blank.

1.   Their ____ are very important to them.

   a. leader   (b.) friends   c. cultural   d. friendship

2.   Could you please give me some ____?

   (a.) information   b. important   c. active   d. suggestion

3.   Maybe we should ____.

   (a.) advice   b. happen   c. show   d. apologize

4.   That information is ____.

   a. brag   (b.) wrong   c. orders   d. argue

B.   Are the meanings of these words similar or different? Write *S* (similar) or *D* (different) on the lines.

1.   _S_ old—elderly
2.   _D_ suggestions—activities
3.   _S_ family—relatives
4.   _S_ overweight—fat
5.   _D_ apologize—brag
6.   _D_ leader—position

Discussion

Talk about your answers to these questions with a small group.

1.   What do men and women in your country say about each other? *Men and women sometimes seem to very speak differen languages in my country*

2.   Are people in your country similar to or different from the man and woman on page 65? *They like to talk about different things. Sometimes they don't listen to each other. A woman makes a*

3.   If you're a woman, what do you talk about with other women? What do you talk about with men? If you're a man, what do you talk about with other men? What do you talk about with women? *suggestion, but her husband doesn't understan*

If I'm a woman, I like to talk about the shopping.
If I'm a woman I am going to talk to a man about the politics.

PART THREE

SCANNING FOR INFORMATION

Here is a wedding invitation. There is also an invitation to the reception and a response card. People use the response card to tell the family that they will come or they won't come.

Complete these sentences about the invitation. Circle the letters of the correct endings.

1. The time of the wedding is

    a. 3:10 P.M.
    b. 3:00 A.M.
    c. 3:00 P.M.

2. The date is

    a. July 8, 1992.
    b. July 18, 1992.
    c. July 18, 1993.

3. The groom (the man getting married) is

   a. Wilson Masker.
   b. Richard Dean Thorne.
   c. Barbara Ann.

4. The last name of the bride (the woman getting married) is

   a. Ann.
   b. Masker.
   c. Thorne.

5. You should answer the invitation

   a. before July 9, 1992.
   b. after July 4, 1992.
   c. before July 4, 1992.

Thank-you Notes

In the United States, when you get a gift, it is polite to write a thank-you note. People usually write about how they will use the gift.

A. Richard and Barbara got many wedding gifts. Write the correct names below the pictures of the gifts.

a blanket	a toaster	a coffee maker
a teapot	a flower vase	a microwave oven

B.   How will people use these gifts? Draw lines to match the gifts and the uses.

1. blanket   a.   to make coffee every day

2. coffee maker   b.   to keep warm all winter

3. toaster   c.   to serve tea to our special guests

4. teapot   d.   to show our flowers

5. flower vase   e.   to make toast every morning

C.   Now practice with a partner. Ask questions and give answers.

Example   STUDENT A: How will they use the blanket?
                STUDENT B: They'll use it to keep warm all winter.

D.   Complete these thank-you notes for the presents on page 69.

PART FOUR

WRITING

A.   Here is a picture story about Henry and Sadae. Look at each picture. Then look at the sentences in the box. Write the correct sentences for each picture.

They were angry at each other.   They got married.
They met.   He never wanted to talk to her about
He asked her to marry him.   work.
They were in love.

1.

They met.

2.

3.

4.

5.

6.

B.   Work with a partner. Ask questions about the story. Ask what happened first, second, third, fourth, fifth, and sixth. You can use the pictures on page 71 to help you answer.

Example   A. What happened first?
               B. They met.

C.   Henry is talking to his friend Angelo about his wife. Complete the sentences. Use the picture and the words in the box to help you.

washed	watched	angry	her
with	TV	don't	is
talk	read	me	

HENRY: My wife *is angry* with _____.

ANGELO: Why?

HENRY: I _____ know.

ANGELO: What did you do last night?

HENRY: Let's see. I _____ for a while, and then I _____ my

        car. Later I _____ a baseball game on _____.

ANGELO: Did you talk with your wife?

HENRY: No, I didn't.

ANGELO: Well, maybe you should _____ _____ _____.

D. Henry's wife, Sadae, is talking to her friend Prinda. Work in a small group. Complete this dialog. There are no right or wrong sentences. Write as many sentences as you can.

SADAE: I'm really angry.

PRINDA: Why?

SADAE: Because Henry _____

_____

PRINDA: Is that all?

SADAE: No.

PRINDA: _____

_____

SADAE: _____

E. Do you have problems when you talk with one of the people listed in the box below? What do you say to the person? What does the person say to you?

　　Write a dialog. You and that person will talk. What will you say? What will the person say?

boyfriend	husband	brother
girlfriend	mother	sister
wife		

6

NATIVE AMERICANS AND IMMIGRANTS

LESSONS FROM NATIVE AMERICANS

Before You Read

Look at the picture and the map.

1. Who are the people in the picture? What year is it?

2. Why is there food in the middle of the map? What are the arrows (⤳) pointing to?

When you read "Lessons from Native Americans," don't use a dictionary. You'll learn to find the meaning of a new word before or after the phrase *and other*. Also, you'll see two ways to use quotation marks (" ").

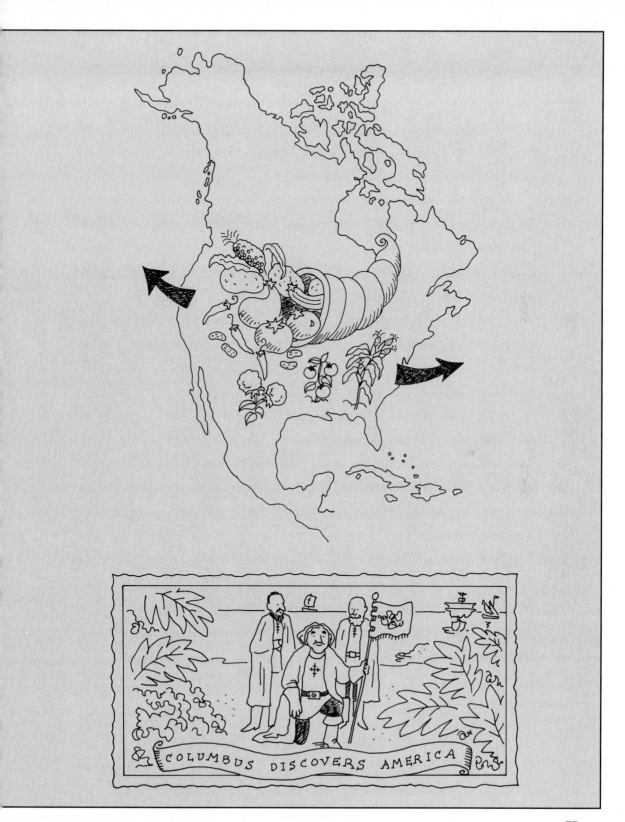

COLUMBUS DISCOVERS AMERICA

Lessons from Native Americans

A   Many history books begin, "Christopher Columbus discovered America in 1492." But how can this be true? Millions of people already lived in the Americas at that time. Columbus was looking for India, so he called the people "Indians." Columbus was wrong.

B   People soon began to come to the Americas from Spain, England, France, and other European countries. These Europeans wanted land. They were afraid of the Native Americans ("Indians"). They killed many Native Americans and took their land. They changed the Native American way of life forever. Most of these changes were terrible.

C   Native Americans changed the world in many ways too, but most of these changes made life better. Today most people know nothing about the clothing, foods, and ideas from the Native Americans of several hundred years ago.

D   Before people from Europe "found" the Americas, Europeans wore wool clothing. Rich people wore silk from China. People in India and the Middle East grew cotton, but it was difficult to make this cotton into cloth. Cotton in North America was very strong. Europeans saw it and thought, "This is silk!" Soon people in all countries, rich and poor, wore cotton clothing.

E   Native Americans changed the world's way of eating too. They grew potatoes, squash, corn, beans, and other vegetables. They had peanuts, hot chilies, and peppers. The Europeans learned about these "new" foods and took them to other countries. Today these are important foods in Europe, Africa, and Asia.

Main Ideas

A.   Circle the number of the main idea of "Lessons from Native Americans."

1.   Columbus discovered America in 1492.

2.   Many things in our lives today came from Native Americans.

3.   Many kinds of food came from the Americas.

B. Read the story again. Every paragraph has a letter. What is the main idea of each paragraph? Write the letters on the lines.

___D___ Native Americans gave the world a good, strong kind of cotton.

_____ Christopher Columbus didn't really discover America, and Native Americans aren't really Indians.

_____ Europeans in North America were terrible to Native Americans.

_____ Many foods in the world today came from the Americas.

_____ Native Americans changed the world in many ways.

New Words

Sometimes you can understand a new word because it comes after the phrase *and other*.

Example   Today we wear cotton, wool, silk, and other kinds of <u>cloth</u>.

What are examples of cloth? *cotton, wool, and silk*

Sometimes the new word comes before the phrase *and other*.

Example   I enjoy Indian <u>curry</u>, Mexican <u>salsa</u>, and other spicy foods.

What are curry and salsa? *spicy foods*

Look before and after the phrase *and other*. Then answer the questions.

1. People came from Spain, England, France, and other <u>European countries</u>.

What are examples of European countries? _____

2. They grew <u>potatoes</u>, <u>squash</u>, <u>corn</u>, <u>beans</u>, and other vegetables.

What are potatoes, squash, corn, and beans? _____

Discussion

Talk about your answers to these questions with a partner.

1. What are important foods in your country? Are some of them from the Americas?

2. What do you know about Native Americans?

PART TWO

A NATIVE AMERICAN TODAY

Native American Life Today

A   Earl Dean Sisto is a Native American. He works at an important university, the University of California at Los Angeles. Most people call his tribe "Apache," but the Apaches call themselves "Ine." Sisto grew up on an Apache reservation, Native Americans' land. The U.S. government "gave" reservation land back to the Native Americans after the whites took North America from them. Sisto visits the reservation once a year. At first, it wasn't easy for him to live in a big city, but now it's not a problem.

B   Sisto worries about his tribe and all Native Americans. The way of life on reservations is changing. Before World War II, clans were important to Native Americans. Clans are very large extended families. They are part of a tribe. Children learned the traditions of their tribe from other clan members. But today clans are not important to many Native Americans. Some don't use their clan names anymore. Now they use English names.

C   There are serious problems on many reservations. Some tribes are doing well, but most are poor. On some reservations, the unemployment rate is very high. Many people don't have jobs. Many people feel sad and angry. The suicide rate is high. Many Native Americans kill themselves. Alcohol is also a problem on many reservations.

D   Why do these problems exist? The problems really began several hundred years ago when Europeans arrived in North America. There were many differences between the Europeans and the many Native American tribes. The Europeans and their children and grandchildren moved west across North America. They brought wars and new sicknesses with them. They took over more and more of the Native Americans' land. The tribes lost their people, their land, and their hope. They lost their way of life.

E   Today many Native Americans are fighting their problems. Some are working to win back their land. Others, like Earl Dean Sisto, are fighting for the children's education. Few Native American children learn about their tribe's traditions at school. Few Native American children go to college. Sisto wants reservation schools to teach the history, language, and culture of Native Americans. He wants Native American children to go to college. They need to understand their past and be ready for the future.

About the Reading

Which of these are problems for Native Americans today? Put checks on the lines.

1. __√__ The unemployment rate on reservations is high.

2. _____ Many Native Americans are at war with other tribes.

3. _____ Today clans are not important to many Native Americans.

4. _____ Some Native Americans are working to win back their lands.

5. _____ Many Native Americans are poor.

6. _____ Many schools don't teach Native American culture to the children.

Some Native Americans live together on reservations. Others live separately on small pieces of land.

Understanding Possessive Pronouns

What do these underlined words mean? Circle the meaning and draw an arrow to it.

1. Children learned the traditions of their tribe from clan members.

2. Earl Dean Sisto is a Native American. Most people call his tribe "Apache."

3. The children need to understand their past.

4. The Europeans and their children and grandchildren moved west across North America.

Building Vocabulary

A. Match the words with their meanings. Write the letters on the lines.

1. __c__ clan

2. _____ reservation

3. _____ unemployment rate

4. _____ exist

5. _____ tribe

    a. Native Americans' land
    b. be
    c. big extended family
    d. a Native American culture or nation
    e. number of people without jobs

B. In this box, there are words from Chapters 5 and 6. Fill in the squares of the crossword puzzle with these words.

easy	friendship	clan	rich
cloth	similar	up	reservations
Spain	corn	million	equal
cotton	die	tribe	kill

ACROSS

1. with a lot of money

3. a big extended family

5. Native Americans' lands

7. not difficult

8. silk, cotton, and wool

10. to stop living

12. not different; almost the same

14. in the same position

DOWN

2. a yellow vegetable

3. a kind of cloth

4. being friends

6. a European country; Madrid is here

9. 1,000,000

11. a group of Native Americans

13. to end (stop) a life

15. Children grow _____.

Discussion

Talk about your answers to these questions in a small group.

1. Are there many people with no jobs in your country? If so, why?

2. Is the way of life changing in your country?

3. Why do you think people on reservations have problems with alcohol?

PART THREE

SCANNING FOR INFORMATION

Reading Maps

NATIVE AMERICANS OF
THE GREAT PLAINS

lived in tepees
hunted buffalo
rode horses

NATIVE AMERICANS OF THE
EASTERN WOODLANDS

fished and hunted
lived in wigwams
used canoes

NATIVE AMERICANS OF
THE SOUTHWEST

lived in adobe houses
grew corn and other crops
made beautiful pottery and
   jewelry

A.   Look at the map on page 82 and then answer these questions. Use short answers.

1.   The Delaware lived in the Northeast, didn't they? *Yes, they did.* _____

2.   The Mohawk lived in the Southwest, didn't they? _____

3.   The Great Plains are in the middle of the country, aren't they? _____

4.   The Hopi lived south of the Sioux, didn't they? _____

5.   The Hopi lived in the Southwest, didn't they? _____

6.   The Zuni lived in the eastern woodlands, didn't they? _____

7.   The buffalo were in the eastern woodlands, weren't they? _____

8.   The Cheyenne lived north of the Zuni, didn't they? _____

B.   Look at the map on page 82 and answer these questions. Use complete sentences.

1.   Where did the Sioux live?

   They lived on the Great Plains. _____

2.   What did they hunt?

   _____

3.   Where did the Zuni live?

   _____

4.   What did they make?

   _____

5.   Did the Cheyenne ride horses?

   _____

6.   Did the Delaware ride horses?

   _____

7.   What did the Hopi make?

   _____

8.   What did the Hopi grow?

   _____

C. Here is another map of the United States. The names of some states and of some cities are on the map. Use this map and the map on page 82 to answer the questions below.

1. Find the state of Massachusetts. Read these sentences. Decide which sentences are true and which are false. Circle *True* or *False*.

   a. The Hopi once lived there.   True   (False)

   b. It's near Maine.   True   False

   c. It's near Wyoming.   True   False

   d. The Delaware Indians once lived there. True   False

2. Find the state of Wyoming. Then read these sentences and circle *True* or *False*.

    a. It's near New York.   True   False

    b. The Cheyenne once lived there.   True   False

    c. It's near Colorado.   True   False

    d. The Mohawk once lived there.   True   False

3. Find the state of New York. Then read these sentences and circle *True* or *False*.

    a. Boston is in New York State.   True   False

    b. The Sioux once lived there.   True   False

    c. It's near New Mexico.   True   False

    d. The Mohawk once lived there.   True   False

PART FOUR

WRITING

Using *Too*

A.   Use these words to make sentences.

1. Sioux / Crow / lived on the Great Plains

    The Sioux lived on the Great Plains.

    The Crow lived on the Great Plains too.

2. Hopi / Zuni / lived in the Southwest

    _____

    _____

3. Sioux / Cheyenne / rode horses

    _____

    _____

Now make two more sentences. Use the map on page 82 for help.

4. _____

   _____

5. _____

   _____

B.   There is another way to write the pairs of sentences in exercise A. Look at sentence 1 below and then write the sentences from exercise A again.

1. *The Sioux lived on the Great Plains, and the Crow did too.* _____

2. _____

3. _____

4. _____

5. _____

Using *Either*

Use these words to make pairs of sentences. With a negative, use *either* in the second sentence.

1. Sioux / Crow / didn't live in the eastern woodland

    The Sioux didn't live in the eastern woodlands. _____

    The Crow didn't live there either. _____

2. Delaware / Mohawk / didn't ride horses

    _____

    _____

3. Hopi / Mohawk / didn't live in tepees

    _____

    _____

4. Sioux / Delaware / didn't live in adobe houses

    _____

    _____

Writing a Story

A.   Bobby Eagle is a Native American. He lived on a reservation for most of his life. What did he do there? Write sentences. Use the pictures for help.

1.   _Bobby lived in a cabin._ _____

2.   _____

3.   _____

4.   _____

5.   _____

Now Bobby lives in the city. Write what he does now.

6.   _____

7.   _____

8.   _____

9.   _____

B.   Bobby has a brother. He lived on the reservation too. Look at the pictures. Then write sentences about Bobby and his brother.

1. _Bobby hunted._
    His brother hunted too.

2. _Bobby didn't smoke._
    His brother didn't smoke either.

3. _____
    _____

4. _____
    _____

5. _____
    _____

6. _____

_____

C. Write a story about Bobby Eagle. Use these two paragraphs in the story. Each paragraph is about one thing. There is a main idea, and there are other sentences about the main idea.

Here are pictures of Paragraphs 1 and 2. Fill in the blanks.

1.   **2.**

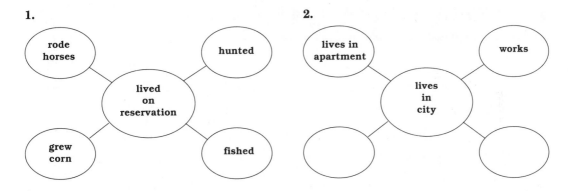

D. Use the pictures and the sentences to write two paragraphs. Use the forms below.

Bobby Eagle is a Native American. He lived on a reservation.

_____

_____

_____

_____

_____

_____

_____

_____

_____

_____

_____

7

WORK AND LIFESTYLES

VOLUNTEERS

Before You Read

Look at this picture.

1. Who are these people?

2. Why are they planting trees?

> When you read "Volunteers," don't use a dictionary. Try to guess the meanings of new words. You won't always understand everything about a new word, but don't worry about it. It's not important to understand everything. In this chapter, you'll learn to find the meaning of a new word before or after a colon (:).

Volunteers

A   Some people go to work each day and then come home. They spend time with their family and friends. Maybe they watch TV or go to a movie. Sometimes they exercise or read. This is their life. But for other people, this isn't enough. They look around their neighborhoods and see people with terrible hardships: sickness, loneliness, and homelessness. Other people see problems with the environment. Many people want to help. They volunteer. They give some of their time to help others.

B   Volunteers help in many ways. Some visit sick and lonely people. Some give their friendship to children without parents. Some build houses for homeless people. Others sit and hold babies with AIDS.

C   Andy Lipkis was at summer camp when he planted his first tree. He began to think about the environment. In many countries, people were cutting down trees. Andy Lipkis worried about this. In 1974, he started a group, TreePeople, to plant trees: pine, elm, cypress, and eucalyptus. Today there are thousands of members of TreePeople, and more join every day. They plant millions of trees everywhere.

D   Ruth Brinker wasn't planning to change the world. Then a young friend became sick. He had AIDS. Soon he was very sick, and he couldn't take care of himself. Brinker and other friends began to help him. In 1985, Brinker started Project Open Hand. This group cooks meals and takes them to people with AIDS. Soon Project Open Hand volunteers were cooking 1,100 meals every day. This number is growing. Ruth Brinker didn't plan to change the world, but she is making a change in people's lives.

E   Twenty or thirty years ago, most volunteers were housewives. They volunteered time while their husbands were working. Today both men and women volunteer. There are volunteers from all social classes, all neighborhoods, and all ages. Most aren't rich or famous. They enjoy their volunteer work. People need them. Today, with problems such as AIDS and homelessness, the world needs volunteers more than ever before.

Main Ideas

Read the story again. Every paragraph has a letter. What is the main idea of each paragraph? Write the letters on the lines.

  _D_ One woman started a group to take meals to people with AIDS.

  _____ Some people give time each week to help others.

  _____ Volunteers help in different ways.

  _____ Different kinds of people are volunteers.

  _____ One man started a group to plant trees.

New Words

Sometimes a colon (:) can help you understand a new word.

Example   There are terrible <u>diseases</u>: AIDS, cancer, and TB.

What are some examples of diseases? _AIDS, cancer, and TB_

(Maybe you don't know all three words: *AIDS, cancer,* and *TB. But don't worry about it!* You only need to know *one* of these three words. It is an example of a disease.)

She cooked some wonderful foods: <u>stews</u>, <u>casseroles</u>, and <u>soufflés</u>.

What are stews, casseroles, and soufflés? _____ *foods* _____

(What kinds of foods are they? You don't know. *But don't worry about it!* You only need to know "foods.")

Look at the words before and after the colon in each sentence. Then answer the questions.

1. They look around their neighborhoods and see <u>terrible hardships</u>: sickness, loneliness, and homelessness.

    What are some terrible hardships? _____

2. He started a group, TreePeople, to plant trees: <u>pine</u>, <u>elm</u>, <u>cypress</u>, and <u>eucalyptus</u>.

    What are pine, elm, cypress, and eucalyptus? _____

Making Guesses

Circle the correct letter to complete the sentence.

The writer probably thinks

a.   volunteers are unhappy people.
b.   people are afraid of AIDS.
c.   volunteers do important work.

Discussion

Talk about volunteers with a small group.

1.   What kinds of volunteers are in your country?

2.   Do you volunteer? If so, what do you do? Where do you volunteer?

3.   What volunteer work is interesting to you?

PART TWO

A SHELTER FOR THE HOMELESS

A Shelter for the Homeless

A Last summer I was a volunteer at a shelter for the homeless, a place for homeless people to sleep at night. I wasn't working that summer. I was taking only two classes in summer school, so I had some free time.

B Three nights a week, I helped in the kitchen of the shelter. With four other volunteers, I planned and cooked a hot dinner for forty-five people. We cooked meals with vegetables, chicken, fish, and fruit. The homeless people needed this good food because many of them usually didn't eat well.

C I enjoyed this volunteer work. The other volunteers in the kitchen were interesting people. We became friends. One was a very nice elderly housewife. One was a movie actor. Another was a young teacher. And the other was a college student, like me.

D I talked to a lot of the homeless people at the shelter. Some of them told me about their lives. Some had problems with alcohol or drugs. But others only had bad luck. One woman worked for almost twenty years for a small company. Then she lost her job. She looked and looked for a new job, but she couldn't find one. She was too old. She needed money for food, so she sold her furniture—sofas, chairs, and tables. The woman still couldn't find a job. She had no money for her apartment. She had to sleep in her car. Then she had to sell her car. She was alone, afraid, and homeless. Finally, she came to the shelter.

About the Reading

One word in each sentence is not correct. Cross it out. Then write the correct word.

1. The writer was a volunteer at a shelter for the homeless last ~~winter~~. *summer*

2. With other volunteers, the writer cooked lunch for forty-five people.

3. The writer talked to a few of the homeless people at the shelter.

4. All of the homeless people had problems with alcohol or drugs.

5. One woman lost her job after ten years with a small company.

Building Vocabulary

Understanding New Words: -*less*

Some words end in -*less*. The ending -*less* means "without."

Example I like sugarless gum.
What is sugarless gum? It is gum without sugar.

A. Write a word for each definition (meaning).

1. She doesn't have a home. She is *homeless* _____.

2. He doesn't have a job. He is _____.

3. They don't have hope. They are _____.

4. He doesn't have a friend. He is _____.

5. She didn't get any sleep last night. It was a _____ night.

6. He doesn't have a heart. (He doesn't care about people.) He is _____.

B. Cross out the word that doesn't belong in each group.

1. tribe   family   ~~place~~   clan

2. sofas   drugs   chairs   tables

3. eucalyptus   elm   cypress   furniture

4. happy   homeless   sick   lonely

5. Native American   Indian   North American   American Indian

6. fruit   corn   squash   beans

7. cook   plan   meal   make

Discussion

Talk about homeless people with the class or a small group.

1. Are there homeless people in your neighborhood? Are there shelters for the homeless in your neighborhood?

2. What are some reasons for homelessness?

3. Does your country have homeless people? Who helps them?

PART THREE

SCANNING FOR INFORMATION

Understanding Volunteer Opportunities

Read this list of volunteer opportunities.

1. *Elder Care:*   Los Angeles Elder Care Corps needs volunteers to visit older people in their homes. Many of these older people seldom have visitors. For information, call Nicky Smith at (213) 555-3444.

2. *Home Building:*   Homes for the Needy builds houses for poor families. They are looking for people to paint and work on houses. Call (213) 555-6777.

3. *Summer Camp:*   East L.A. Summer Camp for Kids needs volunteers. Volunteers will teach sports and games and help the teachers. Speaking Spanish is useful but not necessary. Please call Ramón Martínez at (213) 555-8999.

4. *Blood Drive:*   The American Red Cross needs volunteers. The volunteers will help the nurses. Please call Irene at (213) 555-1112.

Answer these questions.

1. John helped nurses. What organization did he volunteer for?

   American Red Cross
   _____

2. Suzy went to old people's homes and talked with the people there. What organization did she volunteer for?

   _____

3. Ted painted houses. What organization did he volunteer for?

   _____

4. Mary helped a teacher during the summer. What organization did she volunteer for?

   _____

Putting Together a Work History

Ted Parker worked at three places while he was going to high school. He worked for money at Mike's Market, and he volunteered at the other places. He worked at three places for money while he was going to college. He learned something at every job.

Read about Ted. You will use the information about Ted's work history to answer questions later.

TED'S WORK HISTORY

September	High School	June
1983		1987

MIKE'S MARKET	EAST L.A. CAMP	HOMES FOR THE NEEDY
Jan. 1986–June 1986	June 1986–Sept. 1986	June 1988–Sept. 1988
He learned to work a cash register.	He learned to speak some Spanish. He helped the teacher.	He learned to paint houses.

September	College	June
1987		1991

ACE CONSTRUCTION CO.	PEAGREEN COLLEGE LIBRARY	ACME CO.
June 1989–Sept. 1989	Oct. 1989–June 1990	June 1990–present
He learned to use power tools.	He learned to use a computer.	He learned to program computers.

Now match the job title and the place. Draw lines.

JOB TITLE	PLACE
1. painter	a. Acme Co.
2. supermarket clerk	b. Peagreen College Library
3. computer programmer	c. Mike's Market
4. teacher's helper	d. Homes for the Needy
5. construction worker	e. East L.A. Camp
6. library clerk	f. Ace Construction Co.

Understanding a Resume

A resume tells about your education and jobs. Here is Ted's resume. Notice that Ted wrote the earliest dates last. Look at page 98. Fill in the blanks.

Theodore William Parker

1341 S. Beaver Ave., Leavvit, CA 90042

EDUCATION

9/87 to 6/91	Peagreen College	Bachelor of Arts
9/83 to 6/87	U. S. Grant High School	High School Diploma
9/75 to 6/83	Richard Nixon Elementary School	Diploma

WORK EXPERIENCE

6/90 to present	Acme Company	Computer Programmer
10/89 to 6/90	Peagreen College Library	Library Clerk
6/89 to 9/89	_____	_____
_____	_____	_____
_____	_____	_____
_____	_____	_____
_____	_____	_____
_____	_____	_____

PART FOUR

WRITING

Writing a Resume

Complete this resume about yourself.

(Name) _____		
(Address) _____		
EDUCATION		
DATES	SCHOOL	DEGREE OR DIPLOMA
_____	_____	_____
_____	_____	_____
_____	_____	_____
WORK EXPERIENCE		
DATES	COMPANY	JOB TITLE
_____	_____	_____
_____	_____	_____
_____	_____	_____
_____	_____	_____
_____	_____	_____

Using *When*

Look at this sentence.

Andy Lipkis was going to summer camp when he planted his first tree.

One action is longer.   He <u>was going</u> to summer camp.

One action is shorter.   He <u>planted</u> his first tree.

Use the past continuous for the longer action and the simple past for the shorter action. *When* goes before the shorter action.

Use Ted Parker's work history on page 98 to help you write sentences.

1. high school / got a job at Mike's Market

    Ted was going to high school when he got a job at Mike's Market.
    _____

2. college / got a job at Peagreen College Library

    _____

3. high school / volunteered at East L.A. Camp

    _____

4. college / volunteered at Homes for the Needy

    _____

5. high school / got a job at Ace Construction Company

    _____

Using *While*

Look at this sentence.

> Ted learned to work a cash register while he was working at Mike's Market.

| One action is long. | he was working at Mike's Market |
| The other action is inside that action. | Ted learned to work a cash register |

Use the past continuous for the longer action and the simple past for the action inside that longer action.

Now write six sentences about Ted on a separate piece of paper. Use the chart on page 98. Follow the example below.

> Ted learned to work a cash register *while he was working at Mike's Market.*

Writing About Yourself

Write about something you did using the word *while*. Write four sentences on a separate piece of paper. Follow the examples below.

1. *I met nice people while I was staying in Dallas.*
2. *I studied English while I was going to high school.*

FOOD AND NUTRITION

NEW FOODS, NEW DIETS

Before You Read

Look at the pictures.

1. In the first picture, what is the young woman in the middle thinking?

2. What is the young woman in the second picture thinking?

3. How are these two women different? How are they similar?

> When you read "New Foods, New Diets," don't use a dictionary. Use examples and words after dashes (—) to understand new words. Also, you'll learn to guess the meaning of a new word from its opposite.

1.

2.

New Foods, New Diets

A   On March 26, 1662, Samuel Pepys and four friends had dinner at his home in London, England. They ate beef, cheese, two kinds of fish, and six chickens. They didn't eat any fruits or vegetables. Over three hundred years ago, people in Europe ate differently from today. They looked different too. In famous paintings by Titian, Rubens, and other artists, people weren't slender; they were overweight. But people three hundred years ago thought, "How attractive!"—not, "How ugly!"

B   Today people are learning more about health. People in North America and Europe are changing their way of eating. They're eating a lot of fruits and vegetables. Many of the vegetables are raw. They aren't cooked because cooking takes away some vitamins, such as vitamins A, B, and C. People are eating less sugar. They're not eating much red meat. They're drinking less cola and coffee. They're eating low-fat foods.

C   People these days want to be slender, not fat. Sometimes people in North America go a little crazy to lose pounds. Thousands of them join diet groups, go to special diet doctors, or spend a lot of money at diet centers. Each year Americans spend over $30 billion on diets and diet products. Sometimes people lose weight fast, but they usually gain it back again. Almost 95 percent of all people gain back weight after a diet.

D   Diets are changing in a lot of countries, but this isn't always good news. For example, the Japanese diet was very healthful for many years. People ate a lot of fish and vegetables. Now they're eating more and more beef, sugar, and dairy products—ice cream and cheese. This seems similar to Samuel Pepys's dinner party, doesn't it? The problem with this change in diet is easy to see. There is more sickness such as heart disease. The changing diet is not good for the health of the Japanese people.

E   Sometimes people go crazy over food. They eat lots of bad foods because they taste good. Or, other times, they do the opposite—eat very little because they want to be slender. When will people learn? Too much food, too little food, and the wrong foods are all bad ideas.

Main Ideas

A.   Circle the number of the main idea of "New Foods, New Diets."

1. It's important to eat fruits and vegetables.

2. People today eat differently from people in the past.

3. People in the past were fat; people today are not fat.

4. The way of eating today is better than in the past.

B.   Read "New Foods, New Diets" again. Every paragraph has a letter. What is the main idea of each paragraph? Write the letters on the lines.

_*E*_ People sometimes go crazy over food.

_____ Europeans in the past ate differently from today, and they were overweight.

_____ The Japanese way of eating is changing, but the change isn't good.

_____ The way of eating in Europe and North America is changing.

_____ Today Americans don't want to be overweight. They do many things to lose weight.

New Words

A.   Match the words and the meanings. Write letters on the lines.

1. _*f*_ paintings

2. _____ artists

3. _____ diet

4. _____ dairy products

5. _____ heart disease

6. _____ slender

a. way of eating
b. a sickness
c. foods such as ice cream and cheese
d. not fat
e. people such as Titian and Rubens
f. pictures

Sometimes you can understand a new word if you know its opposite. *Big* is the opposite of *small. Terrible* is the opposite of *wonderful.* If you know *one* of these words, you don't need a dictionary for the other.

Example   The people in these pictures weren't <u>slender</u>; they were overweight.

What is the opposite of <u>slender</u>? *overweight*

B.   Write the opposites of the underlined words.

1.   People thought, "How <u>attractive</u>!"—not, "How ugly!"

The opposite of attractive is _____.

2.   Many of the vegetables are <u>raw</u>. They aren't cooked because cooking takes away some vitamins.

The opposite of raw is _____.

3.   They want to be <u>slender</u>, not fat.

The opposite of slender is _____.

4.   Sometimes people lose weight fast, but they usually <u>gain</u> it again.

The opposite of gain is _____.

Making Guesses

Circle the correct letter to complete the sentence.

The writer probably

   a.   doesn't like crazy diets.
   b.   eats a lot of meat, sugar, and dairy products.
   c.   is a member of a diet group.

Discussion

Talk about your answers to these questions with a partner.

1.   How much meat do you eat? How often do you eat fruits and vegetables?

2.   What do people eat in your country? Fill in this chart.

	UNITED STATES	YOUR COUNTRY
BREAKFAST	cereal ham juice *or* eggs coffee toast fruit coffee	
LUNCH	sandwich soup salad *or* salad milk bread	
DINNER	chicken green vegetables potato fruit ice cream	

PART TWO

DIET DAYS

Diet Days

A   My friend Harriet is on a special diet. She's
too thin, so she wants to gain weight. But she
has a problem. She doesn't really enjoy food.
Although it's difficult for her, she eats a big
breakfast every day—eggs, ham, toast, coffee
with sugar, and orange juice. For lunch and
dinner, she eats a lot of meat, dairy products,
bread, and sweets. She doesn't exercise much
because she's afraid to lose weight. But nothing
works. She can't gain weight.

B   I have the opposite problem. I'm overweight, so I want to lose weight. But I have another problem. I *love* food. When I was sixteen years old, I weighed too much. I went to a special summer camp for overweight young people. I lost ten pounds. Then, back at school, I gained fifteen pounds. In college, I went to the Slender Now Diet Center. I lost twenty pounds. Then I gained twenty-four. Nothing works. Maybe I'll never be slender.

C   I put a picture on my kitchen door. It's a picture of a very thin, beautiful woman. I want to look like that. When I see the picture, I should remember my diet and not open the refrigerator. Well, that's the idea. But it doesn't work. I still open the refrigerator and eat and eat and eat. Then, of course, I feel terrible. My friend Harriet has a picture on her refrigerator door. This woman isn't overweight, but she's not skinny. Harriet wants to look like that. But this doesn't work either. So I have a new plan. I'll give Harriet my picture, and she'll give me hers. We won't worry about diets. Good idea?

About the Reading

Which sentences are about the writer? Which sentences are about her friend Harriet? Put check marks on the lines.

	WRITER	HARRIET
1. She loves food.	✓	___
2. She doesn't enjoy food.	___	___
3. She eats a lot of food.	___	___
4. She went to a special summer camp.	___	___
5. She lost weight and then gained it again.	___	___
6. She doesn't exercise much because she's afraid to lose weight.	___	___
7. She has a picture of a thin woman on her kitchen door.	___	___

Understanding Organization

Most paragraphs have one main idea and other information about this main idea.

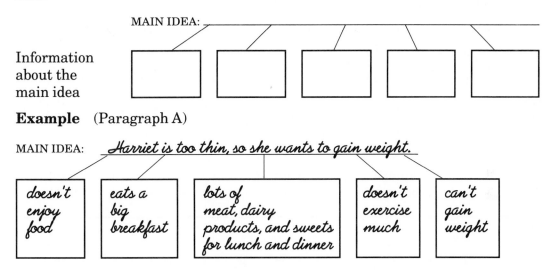

MAIN IDEA: _____

Information about the main idea

Example   (Paragraph A)

MAIN IDEA: *Harriet is too thin, so she wants to gain weight.*

| *doesn't enjoy food* | *eats a big breakfast* | *lots of meat, dairy products, and sweets for lunch and dinner* | *doesn't exercise much* | *can't gain weight* |

Look at Paragraph B. Finish the plan for the paragraph.

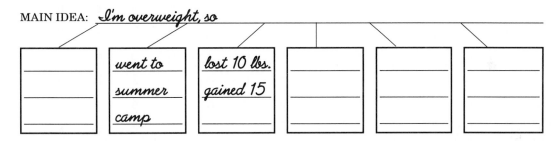

MAIN IDEA: *I'm overweight, so* _____

| | *went to summer camp* | *lost 10 lbs. gained 15* | | | |

Building Vocabulary

A.   Complete these sentences. Circle the letters of the answers. There is one answer for each blank.

1.   I'm trying to _____ weight.

   (a.) gain   b. give   c. be   d. much

2. She has the ___ problem.

   a. too   b. opposite   c. healthful   d. almost

3. We went to a special ___.

   a. heart disease   b. summer camp   c. social classes   d. diet centers

4. He weighs ___.

   a. weight   b. pounds   c. too much   d. healthful

B.   In this box, there are ten words for things to eat. Find them in the puzzle
and circle them. Work quickly.

meal	squash	peanuts	fruit	corn
food	bean	egg	dinner	meat

g	p	f	o	o	d	x	e	p	l	s	r	a	d
x	n	l	e	i	i	z	a	e	y	n	v	m	u
d	c	q	s	w	n	n	p	a	o	t	j	e	n
e	o	r	p	y	n	l	e	n	u	d	h	a	k
r	r	e	l	v	e	m	e	u	l	b	g	t	b
b	n	q	c	k	r	a	o	t	o	m	i	h	j
e	m	p	i	w	o	c	y	s	q	u	a	s	h
a	t	n	s	e	g	g	f	r	u	i	t	f	x
n	p	b	m	e	a	l	e	z	b	l	u	n	a

Discussion

Talk about diets with a small group.

1. Are you trying to gain or lose weight? If so, how do you do it?

2. What foods do you eat?

3. Are there diet centers or special summer camps in your country? If so, tell a
little about them. If not, why aren't there any?

PART THREE

SCANNING FOR INFORMATION

Understanding a Recipe

Here is a recipe for a salad. Read the recipe. If you have problems with any of the vocabulary, ask your teacher for help. Then read the recipe again.

LIST OF INGREDIENTS

1. some tomatoes (5 or 6)
2. a few onions (2 or 3)
3. a head of lettuce
4. a little lemon juice (4 tbsp.)
5. some olive oil (½ cup)
6. a pinch of salt (⅛ tsp.)

DIRECTIONS

1. Cut up the tomatoes and onions.
   Put them in a big bowl.

2. Tear the head of lettuce into a lot of pieces.
   Put them in the bowl too.
   Now you have a salad.

3. Mix the lemon juice and olive oil.
   Add the salt.
   This is the salad dressing.

4. Pour the salad dressing over the salad.

5. Toss the salad.

6. Serve.

A. Complete these sentences. Circle the answers.

1. *Some* tomatoes are _____.

   a. 1 or 2   b.) 5 or 6   c. 10 or 12

2. *A few* onions are _____.

   a. 1 or 2   b. 3 or 4   c. 7 or 8

3. *A lot of* pieces of lettuce are _____.

   a. 3 or 4   b. 6 or 7   c. 20 or 30

4. *A little* lemon juice is ____.

    a. a few tablespoons   b. a lot of tablespoons c. a cup

5. *A pinch of* salt is ____.

    a. a few teaspoons   b. very little   c. a lot

B.   Complete these sentences. Write the correct words in the spaces.

1. He's tearing the _____.

    a. olive oil   b. paper   c. window

2. She's pouring the _____.

    a. tomatoes   b. water   c. bowl

3. He's tossing a _____.

    a. ball   b. house   c. car

4. They're serving _____.

    a. a newspaper   b. a TV   c. dinner

C.   Work with a partner. Ask and answer questions about the recipe. Don't look at the directions. Your partner can help you.

Example   What do you do first?
             You cut up the tomatoes.

Reading Charts

A.   This chart lists the fat and calories in a few foods.

FOOD	CALORIES	FAT (IN GRAMS)
1. beef (steak) (3 oz.)	242	14.7
2. broccoli (3½ oz.)	25	.2
3. chicken (baked leg)	130	4.7
4. cookies (1)	57	3.3
5. french fries (8 large)	200	10.0
6. grapes (1 bunch)	51	.1
7. milk (1 glass)	149	8.1
8. tomato juice (small glass)	41	.1

Here is Bill's dinner. Look
at the picture and answer the
questions below. Use the chart
at the bottom of page 112.

cookies   milk   3 oz. steak   french
                                               fries

1. How many calories does Bill's steak have?

    Bill's steak has 242 calories.

2. How much fat does it have? (How many grams of fat?)

    _____

3. How many calories do Bill's french fries have?

    _____

4. How much fat do they have? (How many grams?)

    _____

5. How many calories does Bill's complete meal have?

    _____

6. How much fat does it have? (How many grams?)

    _____

7. Bill's doctor wants Bill to eat about 500 calories for dinner. Does Bill's dinner
    have 500 calories, or does it have more than 500 calories?

    _____

Here is Maria's dinner. Look
at the picture and then
answer the questions on the
next page. Use the chart at
the bottom of page 112.

baked   broccoli
chicken
leg

                         grapes

tomato juice

1. How many calories does Maria's chicken have?

_____

2. How much fat does it have? (How many grams of fat?)

_____

3. How many calories do Maria's grapes have?

_____

4. How much fat do they have? (How many grams?)

_____

5. How many calories does Maria's complete dinner have?

_____

6. How much fat does it have? (How many grams?)

_____

7. You want to lose weight. Should you eat Maria's dinner or Bill's dinner?

_____

8. You want to eat less fat. Should you eat Bill's dinner or Maria's dinner?

_____

B.   Use this chart of healthy weights to answer the questions on page 115.

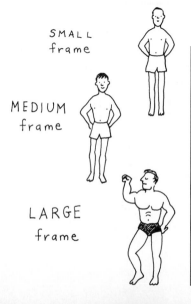

SMALL frame

MEDIUM frame

LARGE frame

height	MEN weight in pounds			height	WOMEN weight in pounds		
	small frame	medium frame	large frame		small frame	medium frame	large frame
5'3"	118	129	141	5'0"	100	109	118
5'4"	122	133	145	5'1"	104	112	121
5'5"	126	137	149	5'2"	107	115	125
5'6"	130	142	155	5'3"	110	118	128
5'7"	134	147	161	5'4"	113	122	132
5'8"	139	151	166	5'5"	116	125	135
5'9"	143	155	170	5'6"	120	129	139
5'10"	147	159	174	5'7"	123	132	142
5'11"	150	163	178	5'8"	126	136	146
6'0"	154	167	183	5'9"	130	140	151
6'1"	158	171	188	5'10"	133	144	156
6'2"	162	175	192	5'11"	137	148	161
6'3"	165	178	195	6'0"	141	152	166

1. Tony is 5′7″. He has a large frame. How much should he weigh?

    He should weigh 161 pounds.

2. Carmen is 5′8″. She has a small frame. How much should she weigh?

    _____

3. Dena has a large frame. She is 5′3″. How much should she weigh?

    _____

4. Daniel weighs 150 pounds. He has a small frame. He is 5′8″. Is he under-weight, just right, or overweight?

    _____

5. Manya weighs 122 pounds. She is 5′4″. She has a medium frame. Is she underweight, just right, or overweight?

    _____

6. How about you?

    _____

    _____

PART FOUR

WRITING

Menus

Bill is eating at Mom's Diner. Mom's Diner gives people a lot of food. The food tastes good, but it is not very healthful. Mary is eating at Lifestyles Restaurant. Lifestyles Restaurant has low-calorie, low-fat, healthful foods.

Look at the exercises on pages 116 and 117, and answer the questions that follow.

A.   Here are parts of a menu. Read each part and answer the questions below.

HUNGRY GUY T-BONE MEAL

You can start with a big, thick steak. We serve it with lots of delicious hot french fries and a cold pickle. Finish with dark, rich chocolate cake and cool, sweet ice cream. Ummmmmmmmmm!

1.   Is this from the menu at Mom's Diner or from the menu at Lifestyles Restaurant?

       _____

2.   List the adjectives in the description.

       _____

       _____

FAT-FREE DELIGHT

This is a big, healthful bowl of wonderful fresh, cold fruit. We serve it with a lot of crisp, green lettuce. A glass of tomato juice comes with the meal.

3.   Is this from the Mom's Diner menu or from the Lifestyles Restaurant menu?

       _____

4.   List the adjectives in the description.

       _____

       _____

B.   Complete this menu selection from Lifestyles Restaurant. Use some of the words in the box to complete the sentences. There are no right or wrong answers.

| fresh | large | crisp | big | very good |
| delicious | healthful | fat-free | excellent | beautiful |

RAIN FOREST SPECIAL

This is a ____, ____ salad. We make it

with ____ fruits and ____ vegetables.

We serve it with ____ tomato juice.

C. Look at the picture of this special dinner from the menu at Mom's Diner. Write a description like the one above.

HAMBURGER PLATE

_____

_____

_____

_____

_____

Recipes

A. Here is a recipe for Maria's salsa. Complete the recipe. If you need help, look at the words in the box below.

a little	some	bowl
a few	an	Put
up	Cut	a lot of

MARIA'S SALSA

1. ___*Cut*___ up _____

   tomatoes. _____ them

   in a _____.

2. Cut _____ _____

   onion, _____ cilantro, and

   _____ chilies.

3. Add _____ salt.

4. Mix it all up.

5. Serve!

B. Do you know a recipe for a salad? Write a recipe and read it to your classmates.

9

TRAVEL AND LEISURE

ADVENTURE VACATIONS

Before You Read

Look at the pictures.

1. What are these people doing?

2. What do you like to do on a vacation?

> "Adventure Vacations" might look difficult, but *don't worry*. You know most of the words. You saw them in Chapters 1 to 8. There are some new words, but try to guess the meanings. After you read "Adventure Vacations," you'll study more about paragraph organization.

Studying the arctic environment

Helping to save the
Mexican rain forest

Teaching language to dolphins

Adventure Vacations

A   People like different kinds of vacations. Some go camping. They swim, fish, cook over a fire, and sleep outside. Others like to stay at a hotel in an exciting city. They go shopping all day and go dancing all night. Or maybe they go sightseeing to places such as Disneyland, the Taj Mahal, or the Louvre.

B   Some people are bored with sightseeing trips. They don't want to be "tourists." They want to have an adventure—a surprising and exciting trip. They want to learn something and maybe help people too. How can they do this? Some travel companies and environmental groups are planning special adventures. Sometimes these trips are difficult and full of hardships, but they're a lot of fun. One organization, Earthwatch, sends small groups of volunteers to different parts of the world. Some volunteers spend two weeks and study the environment. Others work with animals. Others learn about people of the past.

C   Would you like an adventure in the Far North? A team of volunteers is leaving from Murmansk, Russia. The leader of this trip is a professor from Alaska. He's worried about chemicals from factories. He and the volunteers will study this pollution in the environment. If you like exercise and cold weather, this is a good trip for you. Volunteers need to ski sixteen kilometers every day.

D   Do you enjoy ocean animals? You can spend two to four weeks in Hawaii. There, you can teach language to dolphins. Dolphins can follow orders such as "Bring me the large ball." They also understand opposites. How much more can they understand? It will be exciting to learn about these intelligent animals. Another study trip goes to Washington State and follows orcas. We call orcas "killer whales," but they're really dolphins—the largest kind of dolphin. These beautiful animals travel together in family groups. They move through the ocean with their mothers, grandmothers, and great-grandmothers. Ocean pollution is changing their lives. Earthwatch is studying how this happens.

E   Are you interested in history? Then Greece is the place for your adventure. Thirty-five hundred years ago a volcano exploded there, on Santorini. This explosion was more terrible than Krakatoa or Mount Saint Helens. But today we know a lot about the way of life of the people from that time. There are houses, kitchens, and paintings as interesting as those in Pompeii. Today teams of volunteers are learning more about people from the past.

F   Do you want a very different vacation? Do you want to travel far, work hard, and learn a lot? Then an Earthwatch vacation is for you.

Main Ideas

A.   Circle the number of the main idea of "Adventure Vacations."

1. An adventure with Earthwatch is a good way to learn something and have a vacation too.

2. It's more fun to stay at a hotel than to go camping.

3. Disneyland, the Taj Mahal, and the Louvre are wonderful places to see on a vacation.

4. Earthwatch trips are difficult and full of hardships.

B.   Here are the main ideas of Paragraphs A to D. What information about the main idea is in each paragraph? Put checks on the lines.

Paragraph A

Main Idea: People like different kinds of vacations.

√   Some people go camping.

_____ Some people swim, fish, cook over a fire, and sleep outside.

_____ Some people stay at a hotel in a city.

_____ Some people learn about neighborhood problems.

_____ Some people go shopping and dancing.

_____ Some people go to special places such as Disneyland.

Paragraph B

Main Idea: Some people want an adventure.

_____ They want to stay at a hotel and go shopping.

_____ They want to learn something and maybe help people too.

_____ Some groups plan special adventures.

_____ Earthwatch sends volunteers to different places in the world.

_____ Earthwatch volunteers help in shelters for the homeless.

_____ Earthwatch volunteers study the environment, work with animals, and learn about people of the past.

Paragraph C

Main Idea: A group of volunteers is going to study pollution in the Arctic.

_____ The leader is a professor from Murmansk.

_____ The professor is worried about chemicals.

_____ People on this trip will go camping.

_____ People on this trip will ski sixteen kilometers every day.

Paragraph D

Main Idea: You can teach dolphins in Hawaii or study orcas in Washington.

_____ Dolphins can follow orders.

_____ Dolphins understand opposites.

_____ Dolphins are intelligent.

_____ Dolphins are fish.

_____ Orcas travel in family groups.

_____ Pollution is changing the lives of orcas.

New Words

Match the words and the meanings. Write letters on the lines.

1. _c_ go sightseeing
2. ____ go camping
3. ____ tourists
4. ____ adventures
5. ____ orcas
6. ____ volcano
7. ____ pollution

a. the largest kind of dolphins
b. bad chemicals in the environment
c. visit interesting places such as Disneyland, the Taj Mahal, or the Louvre
d. a mountain with fire in it
e. people on a sightseeing trip
f. surprising and exciting trips
g. swim, fish, cook over a fire, and sleep outside

Making Guesses

Circle the correct letter to complete the sentence.

The writer probably

a. likes to go sightseeing.
b. likes adventures.
c. teaches language to dolphins.

Discussion

Talk about your answers in small groups.

1. What do you like to do for fun in your free time?

2. Do you sometimes go camping? If so, where?

3. Do you like to go shopping, dancing, or sightseeing? If so, where?

4. Do you enjoy museums? If so, which ones do you like?

5. Would you like an adventure? If so, what kind of adventure? Are any of the adventures in Paragraphs C, D, and E interesting to you? Why, or why not?

PART TWO

THE TRAVEL GAME

1. Be a part of it. See New York!

2. Visit the Grand Tetons.

3. Explore the coral reef. Go deep-sea diving in the Carribean Sea.

Read the ads for three different vacations. Which one would you like? Write your answer on a piece of paper, *not* in your book. *Don't tell anyone your answer!* Then take this test. Circle your answers. (You'll get more information after the test.)

1. What do you like to do in the morning?

    a. sleep late   b. exercise   c. watch TV

2. What do you like to do on Saturday and Sunday?

    a. go fishing   b. go swimming   c. go shopping

3. What's most interesting to study when you're on vacation?

    a. nothing   b. animals   c. paintings in a museum

4. What do you *not* enjoy?

    a. a busy, crowded city   b. being cold   c. sleeping outside

5. It's boring to _____.

    a. spend the day at the ocean   b. go shopping all day   c. do nothing

6. What gives you a headache?

    a. hot weather   b. smoke from buses   c. cold air

7. What's most important?

    a. clean water   b. clean air   c. a clean bathroom

8. The best food is _____.

    a. cooked over a campfire   b. fresh seafood   c. in a good restaurant

9. I like a vacation to be _____.

    a. quiet, with no worries
    b. exciting, with adventure
    c. exciting, with lots of people

10. Which activity do you like best?

    a. relaxing   b. water sports   c. sightseeing

Making Guesses

Now give your book to a partner. Take your partner's book. Read his or her answers. What can you guess about your partner? In other words, which vacation did this person choose (1, 2, or 3)?

Discussion

Look again at your partner's answers on page 125. Give your partner suggestions. (For example: "You like cities. Maybe you should go to Hong Kong. It's exciting." Or: "Lake Louise is beautiful. You'll like it.")

Building Vocabulary

A.   Which word in each group doesn't belong? Cross it out.

1. skinny   ~~overweight~~   thin   slender

2. breakfast   dinner   dairy   lunch

3. exciting   shopping   dancing   sightseeing

4. organization   team   professor   group

5. eggs   toast   fruit   vitamin

B.   Are the meanings of these words similar, different, or opposite? Write *S* (similar), *D* (different), or *O* (opposite) on the lines.

1. _O_   exciting—boring

2. ____ dolphins—orcas

3. ____ weather—ocean

4. ____ mountain—lake

5. ____ same—different

6. ____ gain—lose

C.   In this box, there are words about travel and the environment. Work with a partner. Fill in the squares of the crossword puzzle with these words.

tourist	trees	trip	travel
adventure	vacation	mountains	orcas
volcano	ocean	pollution	stars

ACROSS

1. an exciting trip

5. time without working (usually 1–2 weeks)

7. high places (such as the Alps, the Andes, and the Himalayas)

10. green things (such as elm, pine, and cypress)

11. "killer whales" or large dolphins

12. a time of travel from one place to another

DOWN

2. a mountain with fire in it

3. If water and air are not clean, there is _____.

4. a person on a sightseeing trip

6. to go on a trip

8. a large area of water (such as the Pacific or the Atlantic)

9. We see them at night, outside, if we look up.

PART THREE

SCANNING FOR INFORMATION

Understanding Travel Information

Read page 129. Don't worry about new words. Look at the pictures too.

A.   Answer these questions about the tours.

1.   Which tour is the most expensive?

   Tour 1 is the most expensive.

2.   Which tour is the longest?

3.   Which tour is the most dangerous?

B.   Answer these questions. There are no right or wrong answers.

1.   Which tour is the most interesting?

2.   Which tour is the most exciting?

3.   Which tour is the best?

C.   Which tour is best for different people? Write the numbers next to these
   travel ideas.

1.   "I just love French food. I want to learn to cook it."   *tour 3*

2.   "I need exercise. I'd like some warm weather too."   _____

3.   "I like adventure. I don't want anything that's easy.   _____
   I'm very healthy."

4.   "I enjoy different cultures. I don't like to see a lot of   _____
   other tourists. I'm interested in Asian cultures."

Now turn to page 130 for more questions about the tours.

Adventure Tours, Inc.

Do you want something different? Something exciting? Here is our new group of tours.

1. TIBET TOUR
Six days in one of the most unusual countries in Asia. Very few tourists go to Tibet. All around are the tallest mountains in the world. You will visit beautiful monasteries and crowded street markets. You will also see wonderful Tibetan dancing.
Length of trip – 14 days. Group size: 16
Cost – $6,000

2. MAUI BICYCLING TOUR
Ride a bicycle around the most beautiful tropical island in the world. You will swim in the clear, warm tropical water, and go camping in the beautiful national parks.
Length of trip – 7 days. Group size: 9–12
Cost – $695

3. COOKING TOUR
Do you like French food? Do you like to cook? Visit Paris and seven other French cities. Visit the best restaurants. Eat the most delicious food in the world. Study cooking with the most interesting chefs of France.
Length of trip – 15 days. Group size: 14–18
Cost – $4,500

4. AMERICAN RIVER TRIP
California's American River is one of the fastest, most exciting, and most difficult rivers to raft. You will never forget this trip! The trip is for adventurous people only! You must be in good health.
Length of trip – 3 days. Group size: 8–10
Cost – $650

5. "I like adventure. I only have three days for my vacation." _____

6. "I love food. I love all kinds of food. And I love Europe." _____

7. "I like to swim and ride my bike. I love to go camping." _____

Using a Travel Map

This is a map of the Boston subway system. There are four lines: the Red Line, the Green Line, the Blue Line, and the Orange Line.

Here are some places to visit in Boston and the subway stops near them.

A.   Use the map to answer these questions.

1. What line is the airport stop on?

It's on the Blue Line.
_____

2. What line is the Science Park stop on?

_____

3. What line is the Symphony stop on?

_____

4. What line is the Kenmore stop on?

_____

5. Is South Station on the Green Line?

_____

6. Is the Harvard stop on the Red Line?

_____

PART FOUR

WRITING

Giving Directions

Give directions. Use the map on page 130.

1. Someone is at Kendall Station on the Red Line. The person wants to go to Haymarket. Give directions.

    Take the *Red Line* to *Park Street*. Change to the *Green* Line. Get off at

    Haymarket.

2. Someone is at Cleveland Circle, on the Green Line. The person wants to go to North Station. Give directions.

    Take the _____. Get off at _____ _____.

3. Someone is at Revere Beach. The person wants to go to the New England Medical Center. Give directions.

Take the _____ Line to _____. Change to the _____.

Line to _____. Change to the _____ Line. Get off at

_____ _____ _____ _____.

4. Someone is at Sullivan Square on the Orange Line. The person wants to go to the airport. Give directions.

_____

_____

Using Comparatives

A. Look again at the tours on page 129. Compare them. Use comparative adjectives.

1. Tibet Tour / American River trip

    a. (expensive) *The Tibet tour is more expensive than the American River Trip.*

    b. (long) _____

_____

2. Maui Bicycling Tour / Cooking Tour

    a. (cheap) _____

_____

    b. (interesting) _____

_____

3. Cooking Tour / American River Trip

    a. (dangerous) _____

_____

    b. (short) _____

_____

4. Tibet Tour / Maui Bicycling Tour

    a. (exciting) _____

    _____

    b. (cheap) _____

    _____

B. What tour or trip do you like? Choose one tour. Why do you like it? Write about the tour on a separate piece of paper. Use comparatives.

Just for Fun

English has many expressions that compare one thing to another.

      He's as big as a house!
      He's as slow as a turtle!

A. Complete these comparisons by adding a noun. Use any noun you want.

1. I'm as hungry as a _____.

2. She's as beautiful as a _____.

3. It's as quiet as a _____.

4. She's as fast as a _____.

B. Tell a partner about your answers.

10

OUR PLANET

THE GREENHOUSE EFFECT AND THE WOMEN OF GUATEMALA

Before You Read

Look at the pictures.

1. Why did someone cut down these trees? How will people use these trees?

2. What problem is the factory causing?

3. There are five kinds of energy here. Which kinds of energy do people use in your country?

The story on pages 136 and 137 might look long, but *you can read it!* You saw most of the words in Chapters 1–9. You can guess the meanings of most new words.

oil

coal

sun

wind

water

The Greenhouse Effect and the Women of Guatemala

A   Most people know something about the greenhouse effect. Factories send gases such as carbon dioxide, or CO_2, into the atmosphere, the air around the earth. In the past, this wasn't a problem because trees absorbed, or drank in, CO_2. But now people are cutting down billions of trees in many countries. At the same time, factories are sending more CO_2 into the atmosphere. It's difficult to believe, but factories put billions of tons of CO_2 into the atmosphere every year! One ton is 2,000 pounds, so this is *a lot* of pollution. There is too much CO_2, and there aren't enough trees, so the world is getting warmer. In other words, we have a greenhouse effect. This is terrible for the environment.

B   What can we do about this? First, we can stop using so much coal and oil. We can learn to use different kinds of energy: the sun, wind, and heat from volcanoes and from inside the earth. Second, instead of cutting down trees, we should plant more trees. One tree can absorb ten pounds of carbon dioxide every year.

C   In the past, the mountains of Guatemala, in Central America, were green and thick with beautiful trees. But people cut down trees for houses. Also, many women cook over wood fires. They walk hours every day to look for firewood. There are fewer and fewer trees, and this is bad for the land. Rain washes good soil down the mountains.

D   Far away from Guatemala, in the state of Connecticut, there is a new factory. The factory uses coal. It will send 400,000 tons of CO_2 into the atmosphere every year. Many people are angry about this. But the factory owners are doing something about it. They are giving two million dollars to the women of Guatemala. The Guatemalans will plant trees in their country. These trees in Central America will absorb the carbon dioxide from the factory in Connecticut.

E   Why Guatemala? Why don't people in Connecticut plant the trees in Connecticut? The answer is easy. Trees grow much faster in Central America than in the northern part of the United States.

F   The trees are good for the earth's atmosphere. They're good for Guatemala too. In small towns and villages in Guatemala, most women are poor and have hard lives. Trees help them in three ways. First, the Connecticut factory pays them to plant the trees. Their pay is corn, not money. The corn is food for their children. Second, these women know a lot about their environment. They know where to plant, when to plant, and what kinds of trees to plant. For example, they plant many fruit trees. The fruit gives them vitamins in their families' diets. Other trees are good for firewood. In a few years, the women won't spend so much time walking for wood. Third, all these trees are good for the soil. Now rain can't wash the soil down the mountains so easily.

G   This plan isn't enough to stop the greenhouse effect. But it's a beginning. The women of Guatemala are helping themselves and helping their environment. As one woman says, "We're planting for our families, for our children."

Main Ideas

Circle the number of the main idea of the reading.

1. The greenhouse effect is a problem in the world today.
2. We should stop using coal and oil and use other kinds of energy.
3. A new U.S. factory is making people angry because it uses coal.
4. Women in Guatemala are planting trees, and these trees are helping the women's families and the environment.

Information About the Main Idea

A.   Which information from pages 136 and 137 explains this idea?

MAIN IDEA: *Trees are good for people and the environment.*

B. Read these sentences. If the information is not on pages 136 and 137, cross out the number. If the information is given, which sentence is it in?

1. Trees absorb carbon dioxide. *One tree can absorb ten pounds of carbon dioxide every year.*

~~2.~~ All trees are beautiful. _____

3. Trees give people fruit. _____

   _____

4. Trees need too much water. _____

   _____

5. Trees give people wood for fires. _____

   _____

6. Trees are good for the land. _____

   _____

New Words

Use these sentences to guess the meanings of the underlined words. Don't use a dictionary.

1. Factories send gases such as CO_2 into the atmosphere.

   What is one example of a gas? *CO2* _____

2. Factories send gases such as CO_2 into the atmosphere, the air around the earth.

   What is the atmosphere? _____

3. Trees absorbed, or drank in, CO_2.

   What does *absorb* mean? _____

4. We should learn to use different kinds of energy: the sun, wind, and heat from volcanoes.

   What are three examples of energy? _____

5. There is too much CO_2, and there aren't enough trees, so the world is getting warmer. In other words, we have a greenhouse effect.

   What happens in a greenhouse effect? _____

   _____

Making Guesses

What can you guess from pages 136 and 137? Circle the letter of the answer.

   a. Trees are important.
   b. Connecticut is in the western part of the United States.
   c. The women of Guatemala are rich now.

Discussion

Talk about your answers in small groups.

1. Are there many trees in your neighborhood?

2. What kinds of energy are important in the United States? What kinds of energy are important in your country?

3. In your country, do people talk about the greenhouse effect? Are there groups (such as TreePeople in Chapter 7) to plant trees in your country?

PART TWO

MY CHANGE OF MIND

My Change of Mind

A   When I finished high school back home in Brazil, I took computer programming classes. I thought, "I can get a good job." But I wasn't really happy. I wanted to do something very different. I was eighteen years old, but I still needed to grow up. So I came to the United States, to California. My idea was to go to college. I wanted to study computer science. I didn't speak much English, so I had to go to an adult school to learn the language. I'm finishing my second year now. In these two years, my whole life changed.

B   In California, I wanted to practice listening in English, so I watched a lot of TV programs. I especially liked programs about the environment. My listening got better, but I began to worry about the land, air, water, and animals. I saw dead animals in oil in Alaska. I saw air pollution in many cities. And I learned a lot about my own country. In Brazil, people are cutting down the rain forests. Most of my friends don't think about the environment. Back home, I never thought about it either.

C   I began to read more about the environment. I wrote letters to environmental organizations such as Greenpeace and the Sierra Club. They sent me *lots* of information! Then on National Beach Clean-Up Day, I volunteered to help. They made me the leader of a team of volunteers on Santa Monica Beach. It was hot, dirty, difficult work, but it was exciting. I met some nice people, and that night I was on the TV news!

D   Next September I'll start college. I have to do this in English. It won't be easy, but now English is so much a part of me! I'm making a big change. I'm going to study environmental science. My special area will be marine mammals—dolphins, whales, and sea lions.

E   When I came to this country, I felt lonely. I cried a lot. Now I'm happy and excited. There I am in the photo above the seals. I'm going to start my new life!

Lourdes Oliveira

About the Reading

Put these actions in the correct order. What happened first, second, third, and so on? Write numbers on the lines.

_____ She came to the United States.

_____ She wanted to practice listening in English, so she watched TV.

_1_ She finished high school.

_____ She'll start college.

_____ She volunteered to help on National Beach Clean-Up Day.

_____ She wrote letters to environmental organizations.

Outlining and Note-taking

You can understand and remember a chapter better if you take notes. One way is to write the main idea and some information about the main idea in an outline. There are different kinds of outlines. Here's one. Finish this outline. (You'll need to look back at pages 139 and 140.) Don't worry about complete sentences. The smaller circles are for information about the larger circles.

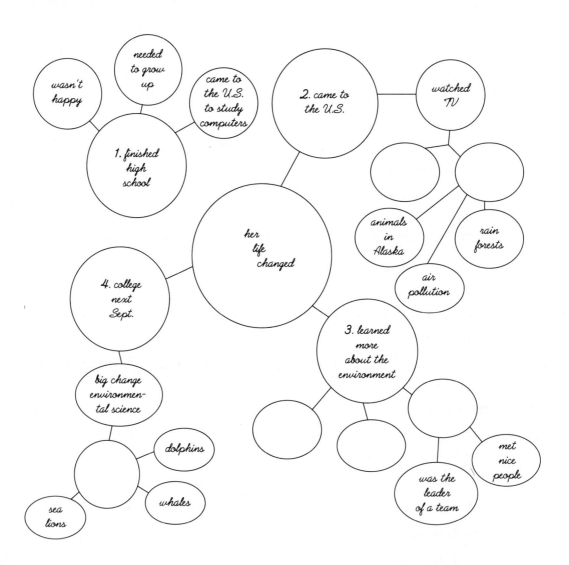

Building Vocabulary

Complete these sentences. Circle the letters of the answers. There is one answer for each blank.

1. He comes from my ———.

   a. Connecticut   b. northern   c. ton   (d.) hometown

2. Let's go ———.

   a. camping   b. boring   c. exciting   d. interesting

3. She wants to study ———.

   a. museum   b. factory   c. rain forest   d. environmental science

4. They ——— some weight.

   a. gained   b. sent   c. stopped   d. followed

5. We use ——— for energy.

   a. ton   b. soil   c. oil   d. mountains

Discussion

Talk about your answers with a small group.

1. Do you watch TV? Does it help your English?

2. Do you write letters in English? To whom? Have you written any letters in English to organizations?

3. When did you come to the United States? How did you feel when you came? How do you feel now?

4. How can you meet new people? Tell about two ways.

PART THREE

SCANNING FOR INFORMATION

Pounds of Garbage Produced per Person per Day

Los Angeles	**6.4**
Philadelphia	**5.8**
Chicago	**5.0**
New York	**4.0**
Tokyo	**3.0**
Paris	**2.4**
Toronto	**2.4**
Hamburg	**1.9**
Rome	**1.5**
Calcutta	**1.12**
Kano, Nigeria	**1.0**

Reading Graphs

A.   This graph tells how many pounds of garbage a person makes on each day in eleven cities. Look at the graph and answer the questions.

1.   Who makes more garbage each day—a person in Tokyo, Japan, or a person in New York?

   A person in New York makes more garbage each day.

2.   Who makes more garbage each day—a person in Toronto, Canada, or a person in Los Angeles?

   _____

3.   Who makes more garbage each day—a person in Calcutta, India, or a person in Paris, France?

   _____

Choose the correct ending and write it in the blank.

4. Five people in Kano, Nigeria, make the same amount of garbage each day

   as _____

   a. two people in Rome.
   b. one person in Chicago.
   c. two people in Toronto.

5. Five people in Calcutta, India, make about the same amount of garbage

   as _____

   a. three people in Los Angeles.
   b. two people in Chicago.
   c. one person in Philadelphia.

B. Mark recycles his metal cans. He takes them to a recycling center so they can be used again. He doesn't throw any out. He recycles his paper products. He puts his yard waste in a pile and puts it on his garden later. Here is a list of what he put in the trash today.

   metal cans: 3 oz.
   food waste: 7 oz.
   yard waste: 0 oz.
   paper products: 2 oz.
   glass bottles, jars, etc.: 4 oz.

Answer these questions.

1. How many pounds of garbage did Mark throw out?

   _____

2. That is the average for what city?

   _____

3. Now how about you? What did you throw out today? Make a list.

   _____

   _____

   _____

C. Tony throws out a lot of things. Today he threw out these things. Use the words below and the graph on page 144 to answer the questions about Tony.

ITEMS	OUNCES
bottles	14 oz.
soda cans and tin cans	8 oz.
1 newspaper, some letters, a magazine	30 oz.
extra food	12 oz.
yard waste	16 oz.

1. How many pounds of garbage did Tony throw out? (16 oz. = 1 pound)

   _____

2. Tony's garbage was exactly average for his city. Look at the graph on page 144.

   Where does Tony live? _____

D. In the United States, many things are in our garbage. Look at the art below and answer the questions on page 147.

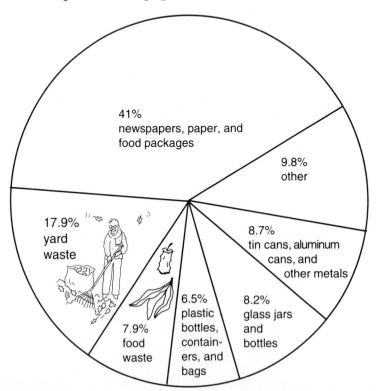

41%
newspapers, paper, and
food packages

9.8%
other

17.9%
yard
waste

8.7%
tin cans, aluminum
cans, and
other metals

6.5%
plastic
bottles,
contain-
ers, and
bags

8.2%
glass jars
and
bottles

7.9%
food
waste

1. What is a larger percentage of our garbage, newspapers or plastic bottles?
   Newspapers are a larger percentage of our garbage.

2. What is a larger percentage of our garbage, yard waste or tin cans?

   _____

3. What is a larger percentage of our garbage, glass or plastic bottles?

   _____

Fill in the blanks.

4. Metal cans and other metals are ___*8.7*___ percent of our trash.

5. Grass clippings and other yard wastes are _____ percent of our trash.

6. Food waste is _____ percent of our trash.

PART FOUR

WRITING

Writing About the Past

A. Think about the day you came to the city you live in. Then circle the answer to complete each sentence. Or, you may complete it any way you choose.

1. I came to this city

   a. this year.

   b. last year.

   c. two years ago.

   d. _____

2. This city was

   a. bigger than my city.

   b. smaller than my city.

   c. the same size as my city.

   d. _____

3. I was

    a. nervous.

    b. excited.

    c. sad.

    d. happy.

    e. _____

4. People were speaking

    a. my language.

    b. many languages.

    c. only English.

    d. _____

5. I planned to

    a. study English.

    b. work.

    c. have fun.

    d. _____

B. Now complete the sentences in this chart. Use the sentences above and on page 147 to help you.

I was _____

This city was

_____

_____

I came to this city

_____

I planned to _____

_____

_____

People were speaking

_____

Writing About Now

A. Think about your life now. Then circle the correct answer to complete each sentence. Or, you may complete it any way you choose.

1. I have lived in this city

    a. only a few weeks.

    b. a few months.

    c. a year.

    d. more than a year.

    e. _____

2. Now I'm

    a. still nervous.

    b. not nervous.

    c. still excited.

    d. comfortable.

    e. _____

3. I speak

    a. a lot of English.

    b. some English.

    c. a little English.

    d. _____

4. I have

    a. a lot of friends.

    b. some friends.

    c. a few friends.

    d. no friends.

    e. _____

5. Now I plan to _____.

_____

B.   Now use the sentences on page 149 to complete this chart.

I speak _____

_____

_____

Now I'm _____

_____

_____

I have lived in this city _____

_____

I have _____

_____

_____

Now I plan to _____

_____

_____

Writing About the Future

A.   Think about your life ten years from now. Then write your answers to these questions.

1.   Where will you be ten years from now?

_____

2.   Will you be speaking English?

_____

3.   What will you be?

_____

4.   Will you remember this class?

_____

5.   Which people in this class will you remember best?

_____

B. Now use your answers to complete this chart.

Ten years from now, I hope
I will be

C. Now use the three pages a[...] [...]hree
paragraphs—one about the [...] [...]out
the future. Look back at pa[...] [...]ng a
paragraph.